CASTE AS SOCIAL CAPITAL

The Complex Place of Caste in Indian Society

R. VAIDYANATHAN

PENGUIN BOOKS

An imprint of Penguin Random House

PENGUIN BOOKS

USA | Canada | UK | Ireland | Australia
New Zealand | India | South Africa | China | Singapore

Penguin Books is part of the Penguin Random House group of companies
whose addresses can be found at global.penguinrandomhouse.com

Published by Penguin Random House India Pvt. Ltd
4th Floor, Capital Tower 1, MG Road,
Gurugram 122 002, Haryana, India

First published by Westland Publications Private Limited in 2019
Published in Penguin Books by Penguin Random House India 2023

Copyright © R. Vaidyanathan 2019

All rights reserved

10 9 8 7 6 5 4 3 2 1

ISBN 9780143459491

Typeset in Sabon by Manipal Technologies Limited, Manipal

www.penguin.co.in

PENGUIN BOOKS

CASTE AS SOCIAL CAPITAL

Professor R. Vaidyanathan is a retired professor of finance who used to teach at the Indian Institute of Management Bangalore. A graduate of Loyola College, Madras, and with a master's degree from the Indian Statistical Institute, Calcutta, he obtained his doctorate from the Indian Institute of Management Calcutta, where he also taught for four years. Prof. Vaidyanathan is a two-time Fulbright scholar and also a fellow of the ICSSR. He was visiting faculty at various universities in the USA and the UK. In the past, he has been selected by *Business Today* as one of the ten best professors at all IIMs. He has had the rare privilege of being on various committees of regulators, like SEBI, RBI, IRDA and PFRDA. He is a consultant to many organizations and is on the board of many corporate firms.

Prof. Vaidyanathan was conferred the Lifetime Contribution Award by the Asia Pacific Risk and Insurance Association (APRIA) and Kybo Life in 2019. His 2013 book, *India Uninc.: Role of Non-Corporate Sectors in India*, which focuses on Indian and Asian value systems, was well received by planners and policymakers. His 2017 book, *Black Money and Tax Havens*, has been acclaimed by experts. Prof. Vaidyanathan is on the advisory council of the Vivekananda International Foundation. He was a member of the National Security Advisory Board under the National Security Council (2019–20). Currently, he is Cho Ramaswamy Chair Professor in Public Policy at SASTRA University, Tanjore, Tamil Nadu, and emeritus adjunct professor at the Rashtriya Raksha University, an institution of national importance located in Ahmedabad.

Celebrating 35 Years of
Penguin Random House India

Dedicated to my granddaughters,
Sanjana and Samyukta

Contents

Introduction

Caste in the Indian Context

The word 'caste' in the Indian context immediately evokes derision and, sometimes, anger. Caste is almost always identified with oppression and discrimination. Anyone talking about caste, even in a mildly positive way, is considered as antediluvian and anti-modern, and treated like a museum piece. By and large, opposition to caste is a stated position among the middle classes and others who have been educated in Western-style educational institutions. Still, when it comes to getting into higher-education institutions or government service, and, of course, for marriage alliances, using caste is more or less the norm. This indicates the complex place of caste in Indian society.

In this book, we are not going to delve into the history of caste or its various interpretations. Instead, we are going to understand an aspect of caste that hasn't received adequate attention—that is, the function of caste as social capital.

Many argue—rightly so—that, originally, caste was not based on birth but on *gunas*.[1] The word 'guna' means virtue, merit or excellence. The word 'caste' is of Portuguese origin, and many argue that the concept of caste, as it has been elaborated, marks an attempt to frame Indian society based on European divisions. Under the original varna system, as Swami Vivekananda said, a person's caste was defined by the qualities or gunas possessed by the individual. A combination of the three gunas, Sattva, Rajas and Tamas, determined the varna of the person: Brahmin, Kshatriya, Vaisya or Shudra. In the Bhishma Parwa and in other stories, there is clear proof of caste being based on the qualities of the individual. Also, it is pointed out that there is a difference between the original idea of the four varnas—namely, scholar (Brahmin), warrior (Kshatriya), businessman/farmer (Vaisya) and worker (Shudra)—and today's idea of caste. In today's context, caste is no longer based on occupation but on birth. For instance, a Brahmin by birth may become a businessman and a Kshatriya by birth may become a college professor, thereby not conforming to their caste-based professions.

In the present day, discussions on caste sometimes lead to caste conflicts. The point to note is that most of these caste conflicts are between one section of the scheduled castes (SCs) and the 'developed' castes under the other backward classes (OBC) category. Large sections of the Indian population, who are legally known as the scheduled castes, prefer to call themselves 'Dalits'. As far as caste conflict is concerned, we hardly come across conflicts between, say, two OBC castes, like the Yadavs and Kurmis in Uttar Pradesh, or the Thevars and Vanniars in Tamil Nadu. One party in these caste conflicts is almost always Dalit—and sometimes, they are Dalits who have converted to Christianity. More on this later.

Throughout this work, we will consider caste as it is practised, based on birth, and as it is observed rather than as it was founded on some theoretical basis. Needless to say, castes are not unique to the Hindu system. Christians, Muslims and Sikhs, too, have their own version of the caste system. More than anything else, matrimonial advertisements reveal this pan-religious aspect of caste in the Indian context. For instance, in Tamil Nadu, demands for Nadar Christian and Pillai Christian grooms or brides are common. There have also been reports that some Christian priests in Kerala refused to conduct the baptism of some fellow Christians—the priests claimed that they were originally 'Brahmins' and hence superior to the latter.

POTA (Pulled Out of Thin Air) Data

In spite of the fact that caste plays such a major role in elections, education and employment in government services, the factual data available on it is meagre.

Hence, most of the arguments are not based on data, but on assertions and emotions.

The last census to enumerate castes in India was undertaken in 1931, after which there has been no census data with respect to caste. The 1941 census was not fully conducted due to the Second World War, and in 1951—after Independence—the government under Nehru stopped enumerating caste in the census, pursuing its goal of a casteless society.

Incidentally, the famous Mandal Commission, which recommended up to 27 per cent reservations for OBCs in Central-government and public-sector jobs, was based on the 1931 census figures extrapolated to the 1980s. And this was implemented in the 1990s. The total reservation was fixed at 49.5 per cent (15 per cent for the SCs, 7.5 per cent for the scheduled tribes and 27 per cent for the OBCs), since the Supreme Court had fixed a ceiling of 50 per cent for reservation. Even this 50 per cent ceiling has been breached by a state like Tamil Nadu—which has as much as 69 per cent reservation—stating historical reasons. Actually, the extrapolation done by the Mandal Commission was not correct in estimating the OBC population. More on this, too, later.

Many demands have been made to have a caste census both at the state and Central levels. While reservation is supposed to be based on social and economic backwardness, in practice it is based on caste criteria, and therefore, a caste census could provide the actual numbers in different castes and help in deciding the corresponding proportions in reservation. There have also been attempts to remove what is known as the 'creamy layer' (richer sections) from reservations, but these have not been very successful.

The latest census, in 2011, was to have included caste categories, but the government of the day felt this was not operationally feasible, and decided to conduct a separate socio-economic caste census and not club it with the regular census. This census has thrown up more questions than answers. The NITI Aayog has been asked to analyse the data, but it is yet to submit its report. We quote from a report on the complexities involved in cleaning up the data gathered by this census:

'Clearly, different people understood different things when they were asked about their caste,' a government official associated with the enumeration exercise that started in 2011–12 told *Hindustan Times* (*HT*), explaining why they ended up with 4.6 million caste entries. That was after the Registrar General of India (RGI) C. Chandramouli flagged problems in the caste data generated by states.

In all, the RGI's office has so far pointed out defects in caste data related to every fourth household: 81 million errors of a total 330 million recorded cases. About 67 million cases were rectified by the states, but 14 million were still pending, a senior government official told *HT*.

That census enumerators who covered 330 million households ended up with a list of 4.6 million entries implying that on average, only seventy-two households used the same phrase to identify their caste. Back in the 1980s, the Anthropological Survey of India had also attempted to classify caste names but had to tone down its ambitious plan.

It was unable to classify the 65,000 castes thrown up by its study—not as comprehensive as a census—and decided to limit itself to identifying 7,331 communities instead.[2]

There have been attempts by some state governments to enumerate castes in their states. For instance, Karnataka conducted an elaborate caste and socio-economic census in 2017. Almost immediately, there was trouble. A news report stated the following: 'According to the census data seen by News18, Dalits and Muslims outnumber Lingayats and Vokkaligas. The SCs account for 19.5 per cent of the total population in the state, making it the single-largest caste entity. Muslims come next, making up 16 per cent of the population. These two groups are followed by the Lingayats and Vokkaligas, who make up 14 per cent and 11 per cent of the population, respectively.'[3]

It was traditionally assumed that the Lingayats and Vokkaligas (two prominent and powerful caste groups) constitute the largest proportion of the population in the state, and this leaked census report turned that assumption upside down. It has since not been released by the Karnataka government.

Given the lack of a caste census, it would not be wrong to say that most of the decisions pertaining to caste-based reservations in education or in government jobs are not based on factual data but on the ability of groups to agitate more. For instance, the demand by advanced agricultural castes, like Jats, Patidars, Gujjars, Kapus, Marathas and others, for reservation in jobs is interesting since many of these groups were ruling kingdoms till Sardar Patel merged more than 500 small and big kingdoms into the Indian Union. We are a unique country where erstwhile rulers want to have the 'backward' tag. Of course, many of these agricultural communities want reservation since agriculture is not very remunerative and employment opportunities are not increasing for them. Reservation, they feel, might enable them to secure government employment and improve their economic position.

The clamour for government jobs is not only due to what is called the 'safety' of the job, meaning job security, but also because these jobs are seen as providing plenty of opportunity for corruption, which is an attractive possibility.

Caste Aggregation

In a sense, some experts are of the opinion that the first census of 1881, conducted by the British, created hierarchy. As mentioned before, the word caste itself is derived from Portuguese *casta*. Indians have typically used the terms 'varna' and 'jati' to denote caste. Of the nearly 2000 castes listed in the 1881 register, the national census report for that year identified only 207.

In the 1881 census, the census commissioner W.C. Plowden decided the five categories into which the castes would be grouped, namely the Brahmins, Rajputs, castes of good social position, inferior castes and non-Hindus or aboriginal castes. The number of castes identified in the 1901 census was 1646, which increased to 4147 in the 1931 census—the last census on caste in India.

However, the total number of castes also included over 300 castes whose religion was recorded as Christianity and over 500 who were recorded as Muslims. In the British census, however, caste, particularly in the case of the Hindus, was not recorded as reported by the respondents. Instead, enumerators were asked to determine the caste status for them.[4]

Further, of the 1929 castes identified in the 1881 census, 1126 (58 per cent) had a population of less than 1000. Two hundred and seventy-five castes had less than ten members, and there were several one-member castes. Of the 1929 castes, 1432 (74 per cent) were found in one locality. Caste/sub-caste/ sub-sub-caste was the order of the day. But post-Independence, the situation changed to the aggregation of castes.[5]

Democracy creates its own fascinating opportunities. The principle of 'one man, one vote' has actually given a fillip to caste aggregation. Earlier, castes used to be atomized into many million sub-castes. Many of these sub-castes were endogamous. But now, due to the power of voting and mass mobilization, caste aggregations are becoming common. Hundreds of sub-castes are subsumed under a broader caste, which, by dint of their numbers, command and demand attention. In Tamil Nadu, three major castes, namely the Kallar, Maravar and Agamudayar, are now commonly grouped together as the Thevars. Earlier, there were close to sixty or so sub-castes among them. But this new aggregation helps them become a powerful negotiating block in the current democratic system. The same is the case with the Jats of Haryana, the Patels of Gujarat and others.

There are two aspects to this caste identification. M.N. Srinivas, the doyen of Indian sociologists, points out, 'An important feature of social mobility in modern India is the manner in which the successful members of the backward castes work consistently for improving the economic and social condition of their caste fellows. This is due to the sense of identification with one's own caste, and also a realisation that caste mobility is essential for individual or familial mobility.'[6]

Traditionally, it is assumed that caste is a rigid hierarchical system which is oppressive. But as the renowned sociologist Dipankar Gupta points out, 'In fact, it is more realistic to say that there are probably as many hierarchies as there are castes in India. To believe that there is a single caste order to which every caste, from Brahmin to untouchable, acquiesce ideologically, is a gross misreading of facts on the ground. The truth is that no caste, howsoever lowly placed it may be, accepts the reason for its degradation.'[7]

What is often forgotten is that caste is used as social capital and a modern tool for upward mobility. Even though the government thinks of providing opportunities to individuals in terms of education and jobs, what is actually happening is the movement of entire castes in terms of their economic and social position. The upward movement of entire castes is part of our study, since caste as social capital facilitates support systems in credit, education, risk mitigation and so on. This upward mobility of entire groups is what is of interest to us in this book.

Outline of the Book

In Chapter 1, we delve into the so-called caste discrimination in education in the past, using the pioneering work of Dharampal in the field of education. In Chapter 2, we explore the current system of reservation in education and how it is not based on scientific reasoning but on political patronage. This has resulted in reverse discrimination. Chapters 3 and 4 deal with caste categories and entrepreneurship. And Chapter 5 discusses social capital as understood in Western contexts. Chapter 6 explores social capital in the Indian context. And Chapter 7 focuses on caste and economic clusters. Chapter 8 explains how the Vaishyavization of India is taking place, wherein all castes are entering business. Chapter 9 deals with caste and the service sector in India, since the service sector contributes more than 60 per cent of our GDP. Chapter 10 discusses the role of caste in politics which has acquired major importance. It is suggested, as a conclusion, that the 2024 general election may primarily be the caste assertion of different segments.

1

Caste and Education

Was There Caste-Based Discrimination in Education?

Whenever caste is mentioned in popular discourse, discrimination is automatically mentioned along with it, and it is emphasized that in education, discrimination was prevalent in the pre-Independence period. This has been the persistent clamour of political parties since Independence. Even prior to Independence, there was a clamour for reservation in education on the basis of the argument that there was substantial discrimination and denial of education to SC, ST and OBC groups in the pre-British period by the upper castes.

Today, the discussion about backward classes, more often than not, has become a debate about backward castes. Typically, 'backwardness' is defined to include social, educational and economic backwardness. But in practice it is identified more with social and educational backwardness, and hence, many castes have been classified as backward and are provided with reservations in institutions of higher learning—particularly in the disciplines of engineering and medicine—in most states. In Tamil Nadu for instance, as previously mentioned, 69 per cent of the available jobs have been reserved for such categories; and one of the major arguments is that the backward castes are educationally backward due to discrimination in the past, and hence they cannot compete with others, which creates the need for reservations.

History Does Not Fully Support the Thesis of Discrimination

The renowned Gandhian Dharampal visited British and Indian archives and reproduced reports of surveys which were undertaken by the British in the Madras Presidency, Punjab and the Bengal Presidency between 1800 and 1830. He also studied British archives in the British Museum. He discovered that a fairly detailed survey of school and college education had been undertaken by the British administration in the erstwhile Madras Presidency area. According to the survey conducted between 1822 and 1825 in the Madras Presidency (that is, the whole of the Indian states of Tamil Nadu and Andhra Pradesh, and parts of Odisha, Kerala, Karnataka and the union territory of

Lakshadweep), 11,575 schools and 1094 colleges were then in existence in the Presidency, and the number of students in them were 1,57,195 and 5431, respectively. Much more important, in view of our current debates and assumptions, is the unexpected and important information recorded with regard to the broad caste composition of the students in these institutions. This data has been detailed in Table 1.1.

Table 1.1
Survey of Madras Presidency on Education
During 1822–25

Share of Shudras in Schools	Percentage
Tamil-speaking areas	70–80 per cent
Odia-speaking areas	62 per cent
Malayalam-speaking areas	54 per cent
Telugu-speaking areas	35–50 per cent
Share of Brahmins in Tamil-speaking Areas	
South Arcot	13 per cent
Madras	23 per cent

Source: Dharampal, *The Beautiful Tree: Indigenous Indian Education in the Eighteenth Century*

As is clear from the table, the position, as early as the first part of the nineteenth century, was significantly in favour of the backward castes (Shudras) as far as secular education was concerned. Hence the British-inspired propaganda, that education was not available to the so-called backward castes prior to their efforts, is not valid. 'Secular' education had always played a major role in social transformation even prior to British rule.

Another report, by J. Dent, secretary, Fort George, dated 21 February 1825, stated that out of 1,88,680 scholars in all the collectorates of Madras Presidency, Brahmins made up 23 per cent while Shudras constituted 45 per cent.

As pointed out by author Sanjeev Nayyar, the economic policies of the British were mainly responsible for the educational mess created in India in the nineteenth and early twentieth centuries. In his view, before British rule, traditionally, educational institutions were funded by revenue contributions drawn from the community and the state. About one-third of the total revenue (from agriculture and seaports) was assigned to what he calls 'the requirements of social and cultural infrastructure (including education)'. Even during political turmoil, this system stayed more or less intact. With the advent of the British, however, the quantum of land revenue was increased, and this adversely changed the terms of payment for communities. The collection of revenue was centralized, and this hardly left any revenue to pay for social and cultural infrastructure.

Furthermore, the introduction of European goods greatly diminished the means of the manufacturing classes (small-scale enterprises, or small and medium enterprises [SMEs] in today's parlance). Craftsmen, especially those employed in the weaving of cloth, the manufacture and mining of metals and construction work, were reduced to a state of penury.

In such a situation where funds were scarce, both educational institutions and the manufacturing classes became history, leading to grave consequences. Literacy and knowledge among the Indian people were seriously affected. The traditional Indian social balance, in which persons from all sections of society appear to have received a significant degree of schooling, was also destroyed. This destruction, along with the concomitant economic plunder, led to great deterioration in the status, socio-economic conditions and personal dignity of those now known as the scheduled castes. To a lesser degree, the peasants (largely, today's backward castes) were also affected.

Towards the end of the nineteenth century, various factions did begin to attempt a reversal of the results of British policy. This led to what are now termed as backward-caste movements. What is important to note is that the backward status they were struggling against was not an ancient phenomenon, as usually depicted. Their cultural and economic backwardness (this is, of course, distinct from their status in religious rituals on specific occasions) is post-1800, and what all such movements are basically attempting to achieve is the restoration of the position, status and rights of these people prior to 1800.[1]

It is also interesting to note that even in ancient times women had as much access to education as men. As rightly observed by Nanditha Krishna:

Seventeen of the seers to whom the hymns of the Rig Veda were revealed were women— rishikas and brahmavadinis. They were Romasa, Lopamudra, Apata, Kadru, Vishvavara, Ghosha, Juhu, Vagambhrini, Paulomi, Jarita, Shraddha- Kamayani, Urvashi, Sharnga, Yami, Indrani, Savitri and Devayani. The Sama Veda mentions another four: Nodha (or Purvarchchika), Akrishtabhasha, Shikatanivavari (or Utararchchika) and Ganpayana. In the Vedic period, female brahmavadinis (students) went through the same rigorous discipline as their male counterparts, the brahmacharis. The Brihadaranyaka Upanishad describes a ritual to ensure the birth of a daughter who would become a pandita (scholar). The Vedas say that an educated girl should be married to an equally educated man. Girls underwent the upanayana or thread ceremony, Vedic study and savitri vachana (higher studies). Panini says that women studied the Vedas equally with men. According to the Shrauta and Grihya Sutras, the wife repeated the Vedic mantras equally with their husbands at religious ceremonies. The Purva Mimamsa gave women equal rights with men to perform religious ceremonies. Vedic society was generally monogamous, and women had an equal place.[2]

The current debate also does not take into account that backwardness is not a static phenomenon but a dynamic one. Incidentally, one of the arguments given in favour of reservation is regarding enhancing the 'social status' of these segments. Social backwardness, it is pointed out, is a valid reason for caste-based reservations compared to reservations based on, say, economic criteria.

The sociologist M.N. Srinivas spoke of the manner in which successful members of the backward castes worked to improve the economic and social condition of their caste brethren from a sense of identification with their caste, and also due to the realization that caste mobility was essential for individual or familial mobility. It is also assumed that caste is a rigid hierarchical system which is oppressive. But as mentioned in the introduction, the sociologist Dipankar Gupta has pointed out that there were probably as many hierarchies as there were castes in India, and so to believe that there was a single caste order to which every caste, from Brahman to untouchable, acquiesced ideologically, is a misreading of the ground realities.

So, the widespread notion that discrimination in opportunities for education existed for millennia is a dangerous misconception that clouds our policies and threatens the real progress of the backward castes.

Maybe the time has come for us to question many of the beliefs and myths perpetuated in this discussion on educational backwardness. Politics does play a major role in shaping the perceptions of the common man, but it is the duty of the academicians and other experts to look at issues more dispassionately, so that the future of the educational enhancement of our country is not impaired by mythical dogmas. An important aspect here is the success of India in the software and other knowledge-related industries in the recent past, compared to traditional manufacturing industries, which require more institutions of higher learning that are not governed by perceptions regarding the past. The answer lies in the 'inquiring mind' endowed with ancient wisdom that looks at the past dispassionately and provides opportunities to disadvantaged sections based on facts and not on the basis of myths.

2

Reservation in Education: Weak Data Base

Originally, the idea of OBC reservations was conceived to compensate for educational, social and economic backwardness. The focus was to be on backward classes rather than on backward castes. But, in practice, the focus has been on backward castes, and hence many castes have been classified as backward and given reservation in institutions of higher learning—particularly in engineering and medicine—in most states. One of the major arguments for reservation is that since the backward castes are educationally backward due to discrimination in the past, they cannot compete with others, and hence there is a need for reservations.

1931 May Not Reflect the Reality of 2018

As previously mentioned, the Mandal Commission formula of the 1980s, which allocated 50 per cent of the seats in government service and educational institutions to OBCs, was based on the census data of 1931. The census was affected by the Second World War in the year 1941, and from 1951 onwards collection of caste data (except that pertaining to SC/ST data) in our census count was stopped, since it was felt that such data might not be appropriate in achieving our aim of creating a casteless society.

The assumption made by the Mandal Commission, based on the 1931 census and other parameters, that more than 50 per cent of the population belongs to OBCs, may not be true any longer. On that assumption, the figure of 27 per cent reservation for OBCs was arrived at, which, along with 22.5 per cent reservations for SCs and STs adds up to 49.5 per cent reservation, which is lower than the suggested ceiling of 50 per cent by the Supreme Court. The National Sample Survey (NSS) 2003 (59th round) suggests that the OBCs may only constitute around 36 per cent of the population and not 50 per cent, as was assumed earlier.[1] If one excludes Muslim OBCs, then the figure falls to 32 per cent, according to the NSS. The National Family Health Survey (NFHS) conducted in 1998 suggests that the population of OBCs (non-Muslims) is around 32 per cent, which is fairly close to the NSS figures.[2]

Hence, the earlier assumption regarding the OBC population being around 50 per cent may be a substantial overestimation. In other words, we do not have a reliable headcount for the OBCs, except some counts made by state-level backward class commissions, which are not census-like in their rigour. It may be useful, therefore, to have a detailed caste-wise census to look at the actual numbers.

Current Data Reveals Changes

Let us now look at the data more carefully. Many students who made it to the seven Indian Institutes of Technology (IITs) and other engineering colleges in the last decade and a half have benefitted from reservation. Also, according to a new study that says affirmative action policy in higher education works largely as intended, about 26 per cent male and 35 per cent female students from India's most disadvantaged castes and tribes study in 245 engineering colleges around the country, and they would not have been there without reservation.[3] But still, there is also the criticism that only the 'creamy layer' among the backward castes enjoys the benefits of reservations. Some suggest that only the top 5 per cent of these castes benefit from reservations.[4]

Jayaprakash Narayan, who is from the IAS cadre and is the founder of the Lok Satta movement and the Foundation for Democratic Reforms, is more forthcoming in saying, 'In most selections to/in premier institutions in higher education or recruitment to high-end jobs, it is the children of Indian Administrative Service, Indian Police Service officers and other senior officials, the progeny of Members of Legislative Assemblies (MLA), Members of Parliament (MP) and the other political elite, and the offspring of successful professionals and businessmen who dominate the scene in communities eligible for reservations.'[5]

There are detailed studies about higher education and reservation which point to reasonable representation of OBCs on an all-India level. A study by the Indian Institute of Management Ahmedabad (IIMA) suggests that at the all-India level, the deficit for Hindu OBCs and, to some extent, for Hindu STs is not very high, particularly when one looks at the population that is currently studying or is eligible. The share of Hindu OBCs is 25.6 per cent among the total graduates in the age group of 22–35 years; their share is even higher (28.2 per cent) among persons currently studying.[6]

It is also pertinent to point out that post 2008, when IITs/IIMS started reservations for OBCs at 27 per cent (reservation was already in place for SCs at 15 per cent and STs at 7.5 per cent), it is observed that substantial portions of the so-called open quota of 50 per cent were also fulfilled by OBCs. It should also be noted that this is not set off against the OBC quota in reservation. In other words, the number of reserved candidates fulfilling criteria for the unreserved seats increase the total number of reserved candidates in admission. For instance, a report suggests that as early as 2014, 'Candidates from the Other Backward Classes (OBCs) have broken the reservation barrier this year—4,085 have made it to the common merit list, that is without any relaxation, as against 2,641 seats available for them.'[7]

People in states like Tamil Nadu, which has had reservations from the late 1920s in some form or other, have benefitted significantly due to reservations. For instance, according to a report in *The Hindu* in 2004, students belonging to the backward classes (BCs) or most backward classes (MBCs) bagged 952 of the total 1224 seats (77.9 per cent) in the twelve government medical colleges in the state. The first fourteen ranks in the medical admissions test also went to BC and MBC students. Also, in the open competition category in 2004, five SC candidates were selected for the MBBS course.[8]

In Tamil Nadu, BCs get 30 per cent reservation in educational institutions, MBCs get 20 per cent, SCs get 18 per cent and STs have 1 per cent. Out of the 1224 medical seats in 2004, reserved seats numbered 354 for BCs, 247 for MBCs, 226 for SCs and thirteen for STs. The rest of the 384 seats were allowed as open competition, where everyone competed regardless of community.

The final tally (original list accounting for 69 per cent reservation) released by the Directorate of Medical Education showed that only twenty-eight students from the 'non-reserved' or forward castes (FCs) got into government medical colleges, representing about 2.3 per cent of the total. In fact, among the top 400 rank holders, only thirty-one were from the FCs. Among the top 100 rank holders, only six were from the FCs, seventy-nine were from the BCs and thirteen from the MBCs.[9]

The following analysis is based on the data provided by the Tamil Nadu Department of Health and Family Welfare and the detailed list presented therein.[10] An extract from an analysis of the data for 2015–16, which reveals that the situation has significantly 'worsened' for the so-called forward castes, is presented below:

In 2015–16, Tamil Nadu had 2655 medical seats— including the ones surrendered by private colleges. Out of this, 15 per cent, that is, 398 seats, were filled in via All-India Pre-Medical Test (AIPMT) (which was cancelled after a paper leak).

Key Findings

- It appears that over 95.4 per cent of the population of Tamil Nadu is covered in reserved categories. This is supported by the fact that only 4.7 per cent of those who applied for MBBS are from the general category (forward castes) and that, typically, becoming a doctor is something that forward castes ought not to be interested in.
- The castes classified as OBC have showed absolutely no evidence of disability. Thirteen of the seventeen tied at 100 per cent are BCs.
- There is an urgent necessity to revise the OBC Caste List due to the fact that 72.1 per cent of the open-category seats are taken by candidates belonging to castes currently classified as OBC in Tamil Nadu.

- Only seventy-nine of 4238 doctors were from the general category in 2021–22 (see table below).
- Only fifty-three of 2257 who apply for 100-odd open-category post-graduate seats in 2020 are from the general category.[11]

In 2017, a judge of the Madras High Court suggested some reservation for the poor among forward castes. 'Of 822 [31 per cent medical] seats available in open competition, not only forward community students but also students from other reserved categories are allotted seats on merit. In the process, only 194 seats reached students belonging to forward communities which are equivalent to 7.31 per cent,' the judge said.[12]

We find that Tamil Nadu has a sort of reverse discrimination—since a substantial portion of the so-called open quota is also taken by the reserved category students of OBCs and SCs. Actually, there is a crying need to redefine OBCs and SCs in Tamil Nadu based on their socio-economic conditions and performance.

As of now, nearly 91 per cent of the state's population is classified as backward, to be eligible for 69 per cent of the reservation. We also find that even though 31 per cent is supposed to be available for other communities (OCs), after 69 per cent of the seats are reserved for OBCs and others, in practice, a large proportion of the 'open category' seats are also taken by OBC students.

The data for the National Eligibility cum Entrance Test (NEET) in Tamil Nadu for the last few years reveals a decline in the number of OC seats in the open quota. The figures show that the 'upper castes' got only 1.9 per cent of the open seats out of the 31 per cent.[13]

YEAR	OC	BC	BCM	MBC/DNC	SC	SCA	ST	TOTAL
2017–18	192	1154	133	644	424	78	27	2652
2018–19	155	1171	110	604	404	76	25	2545
2019–20	107	1384	131	685	443	83	29	2862
2020–21	106	1479	152	812	505	94	32	3180
2021–22	79	1990	204	1130	670	123	42	4238

OC: *other communities*; BC: *backward classes*; BCM: *backward-class Muslims*; MBC/DNC: *most backward classes/denotified communities*; SC: *scheduled castes*; SCA: *scheduled-caste Arunthathiyar*

Unfortunately, the caste categories are frozen in reservations and rarely relooked at, even after decades. Not only that, even at the school level, we find that the performance of SCs, STs and OBCs is no less than that of other castes in some states. For instance, take the example of Gujarat. The Gujarat government has released the detailed composition of the various categories for 2010 in class X. Gujarat is a state that has a large percentage of tribes in its population.

The data (see Table 2.2) does not reveal any significant difference between the different social categories. This could be due to the extra coaching undertaken for weaker sections and also due to the sustained campaign to enrol and train female students from weaker sections over a long period.

Table 2.1
Total Number of Candidates for 2257 Seats

	2013–14	2013–14	2015–16	2015–16
TOTAL	28785	100 per cent	31525	100 per cent
BC	12131	42.1 per cent	12944	41 per cent
MBC	6464	22.4 per cent	6754	21.4 per cent
BC Muslim	1518	5.2 per cent	1690	5.4 per cent
SC	6007	20.9 per cent	7257	23.0 per cent
SC Arunthathiyar	966	3.4 per cent	1079	3.4 per cent
ST	211	0.7 per cent	308	0.9 per cent
Open Category (FC)	1488	5.1 per cent	1493	4.7 per cent

Source: *https://realitycheck.wordpress.com/2015/06/21/analysis-of-tamilnadu-mbbs-admissions-2015-16*   *and*   *http://www.tnhealth. org/index.php*

The Dropout Rate Has Reduced

The dropout rate at the elementary level (classes I to VIII) used to be very high among all and more so among SC and ST students, particularly among girls, as seen in Table 2.3.

But we find that there has been substantial reduction in the dropout rates over a period, and this augurs well for redefining the definition of backwardness. Hence, a good grounding at the school level facilitates better performance at the higher levels.

Another aspect, as suggested by many experts, is that there is a need to closely look at the creamy layer among the OBCs and eliminate them from getting the benefits of reservation. One suggestion has been to provide benefits for up to three generations for disadvantaged groups and not beyond.

Table 2.2
Pass Percentage in Class X in 2010, Category-Wise

	SC	ST	OBC	Others
Students appeared	29,594	45,596	1,25,830	1,50,124
Students passed	23,873	39,231	1,08,876	1,29,689
Pass percentage	80.66%	86.04%	86.52%	86.38%

Source: Times of India, Ahmedabad, 28 May 2010

Table 2.3
Drop-out Rate Among Class I to VIII Students
(in per cent)

Year	All Boys	All Girls	SC Boys	SC Girls	ST Boys	ST Girls	Total
1990–91	59.1	65.1	64.3	73.2	75.7	82.2	60.9
2002–03	52.2	53.5	58.2	62.2	66.9	71.2	52.8
2007–08	43.7	41.3	53.6	51.1	62.6	62.3	42.8
2014–15	8.4	8.6	8.1	8.9	16.0	16.8	8.1

Source: Select Education Statistics, Ministry of HRD, Government of India, IndiaStat.Com, Statistics of School Education

Reservation in Jobs

The reservation system is also followed in government jobs, and it leads to similar situations of OBCs getting larger share of 'open category' seats other than the quota available to them. For instance, from the list of candidates selected for the post of junior telecom officers in Bharat Sanchar Nigam Limited (BSNL) under the Tamil Nadu Telecom Circle, using GATE Score, nearly thirty OBC candidates have got the forty-nine seats (non-quota) meant for OCs, apart from the twenty-five exclusively reserved for the OBCs. The OBCs get fifty-five seats against the twenty-five reserved for them, whereas the actual OC candidates are left with just nineteen out of forty-nine. This is because there is no set-off of the OBCs selected under the open or merit quota.[14]

In conclusion, we find that affirmative action, as suggested by the Mandal Commission and implemented by the Government of India, suffers from a lack of reliability of data. The commission used the 1931 census to project for 1980 and arrived at a figure of 50 per cent for OBCs. Available evidence suggests that it may be an overestimate, since OBCs may only be around 30 per cent of the population based on other studies and surveys. Also, many state governments have classified large portions of the population as backward, for reservation in educational institutions, and this has created a peculiar situation wherein even in the open quota there are a number of candidates belonging to the OBCs. Equally important is school enrolment and performance. We find that the dropout rate at school levels have significantly declined among the SC/ST categories (in classes I to VIII). We also find that the performance of weaker sections has been impressive in states like Gujarat.

The position of SCs, STs and OBCs in the sphere of education has shown improvement over the last two decades. In that context perhaps, the time has come to delete the 'creamy layer' among these groups from reservation, so that the bottom of the pyramid gets more encouragement.

We will link this aspect with entrepreneurship later.

3

Caste Categories and Entrepreneurs

A debate is currently raging in the polity regarding reservations for SCs and STs in the private sector, similar to the one that is provided in the government and the public sector. Currently, the private corporate sector constitutes a relatively small portion of the national income, around 15–18 per cent.

As far as employment statistics pertaining to the private sector are concerned, we do not have separate statistics on the numbers employed by the private corporate sector, and proprietorship and partnership (P&P sector) forms of organizations in the private sector. Many companies do not provide information on the number of people employed by them, since these details are not required to be given in their annual reports. Therefore, this chapter is based on what figures are available, even though they may not present the complete picture.

Government and Private Organized Sector

First, the facts. We have provided, in Table 3.1 (for select years), the number of persons employed in government and semi-government organizations. We find that employment in the government and public sector has stagnated since the '90s and has actually shown a minor decline between 2010 and 2012. The reasons are twofold.

One pertains to the non-expansion of governmental activities, particularly in relation to the public sector, as compared to the socialistic approach of the '60s, when everything, from bread to rockets, was made by the government. The second reason is that the government is broke, and more so at the state level. Salary, wages and pensions constitute more than 50 per cent of the expenses of many state governments. Governments (both Centre and states) have shifted from defined benefit to defined contribution pension schemes. The dependency ratio (namely, the number retired to the number currently employed) is increasing at an exponential rate in most governments and government departments. Hence, the opportunity for employment in the government has been significantly reduced.

Table 3.2 gives employment data for the private organized sector for select years. According to the Government of India, as claimed in the Economic

Survey, there were 6 lakh persons employed in trade activities (wholesale and retail) in 2012 in the whole country. This presumably includes hotels and restaurants also, since data on hotels and restaurants are not separately provided and they come under the trade category in official statistics. Also, the number of people employed by the construction industry is stated to be 1.3 lakh across the whole country in 2012. According to the figures, in the transport, storage and communications sector, only 2.1 lakh persons were employed across the whole country in 2012. (These numbers do seem incredibly low! In a city like Bangalore itself, there are probably more than 1 lakh people working in construction activities.) Going by official figures, the government and private organized sectors have only a small share (6 per cent) of the total workforce of the country. The organized private sector employs a total of 119 lakh people, which is around 2.5 per cent of the total workforce of nearly 474 million (47.41 crore) according to the National Sample Survey Office (NSSO), 2011–12.[1]

Table 3.1

Employment as on 31 March (In Lakhs)

Year	1981	1990	1995	2000	2005	2010	2011	2012
Central government	31.95	33.97	33.95	32.73	29.38	25.52	24.63	25.2
State governments	56.76	69.79	73.55	74.60	72.02	73.53	72.18	71.8
Quasi government	45.76	61.73	65.20	63.26	57.48	58.68	58.14	58.0
Local bodies	20.37	22.23	21.97	22.55	21.18	20.89	20.53	21.1
Total	154.84	187.72	194.67	193.14	180.07	178.62	175.48	176.1

Source: Various issues of the Economic Survey till 2016–17, Ministry of Finance, Government of India

Table 3.2

Employment in the Organized Private Sector by Industry (In Lakhs)

Year	1981	1990	1995	2000	2005	2010	2011	2012
Manufacturing	45.45	44.57	47.06	50.85	44.89	51.84	53.97	55.3
Construction	0.72	0.68	0.53	0.57	0.49	0.91	1.02	1.3
Wholesale, retail trade	2.77	2.91	3.08	3.30	3.75	5.06	5.46	6.0
Transport, storage	0.60	0.52	0.58	0.70	0.85	1.66	1.89	2.1
Finance and insurance	1.96	2.39	2.93	3.58	5.23	15.52	17.18	19.1
Community, social services	12.22	14.60	16.03	17.23	18.20	21.40	23.50	24.5
Total (including others)	73.95	75.82	80.59	86.46	84.52	107.87	114.22	119.4

Note: Refers to establishments in the private sector employing ten or more persons. Coverage in construction and trade, particularly, is known to be inadequate

Source: Various issues of the Economic Survey till 2016–17, Ministry of Finance, Government of India

Therefore, under the circumstances, even if the entire organized private sector is reserved for the SC, ST and OBC categories, the gains from employment will be very meagre. But, perhaps, the need is for a different perspective. The more pertinent issue is the share of the SC, ST and OBC categories in the ownership of the private sector.

We do not have continuous data on the said categories post 2012. The Economic Survey has stopped giving out such data. But we have aggregate data about formal and informal sectors in employment. [2]

Formal–informal employment (PS + SS)[3] across the organized and unorganized sectors is given in Table 3.3. Of the additional workers who joined in 2019–20, close to 90 per cent were in the informal nature of employment and more than 98 per cent were in the unorganized sector. About 91 per cent of additional workers were in the unorganized–informal sector. Table 3.3 also gives estimates of total employment in formal and informal categories across the organized and unorganized sectors.

Table 3.3
Formal–Informal Employment (PS + SS) across Organized and Unorganized Sector (In Crores)

Type of Employment	Organized	Unorganized	Total
2017–18			
Formal	4.43	0.28	4.70
Informal	4.62	37.79	42.43
Total	9.05	38.07	47.13
2018–19			
Formal	4.91	0.45	5.35
Informal	4.55	38.87	43.43
Total	9.46	39.32	48.78
2019–20			
Formal	5.09	0.80	5.89
Informal	4.46	43.19	47.64
Total	9.55	43.99	53.53

Source: Estimated using Periodic Labour Force Survey (PLFS) 2017–18, 2018–19 and 2019–20

Note: As per the National Commission for Enterprises in Unorganized Sector (NCEUS) classification, 'The unorganised sector consists of all unincorporated private enterprises owned by individuals or households engaged in the sale and production of goods and services operated on a proprietary or partnership basis and with less than ten total workers.'

We also have industry-wise information for the years 2018–19 and 2019–20 from the Economic Survey 2021–22.[4] The industry-wise employment (PS + SS) in India is given in Table 3.4. Of the workers added in 2019–20, as the table shows, more than 71 per cent were in the agriculture sector. Among the new workers in the agriculture sector, females accounted for about 65 per cent. The trade, hotel and restaurant sector accounted for a little over 22 per cent of the new workers, in line with the 2018–19 trend, where the sector represented more than 28 per cent of the new workers. The share of manufacturing declined from 5.65 per cent of new workers added in 2018–19 to about 2.41 per cent of new workers added in 2019–20; the same trend was witnessed in construction, which recorded a decline from 26.26 per cent to 7.36 per cent.

Table 3.4
Industry-Wise Employment (PS + SS) in India (In Crores)

Year/Sector	Rural			Urban			Total		
	Male	Female	Total	Male	Female	Total	Male	Female	Total
2018–19									
Agriculture	12.97	6.01	18.98	0.62	0.26	0.88	13.58	6.27	19.86
Mining & quarrying	0.10	0.02	0.11	0.08	0.01	0.08	0.17	0.02	0.20
Manufacturing	1.78	0.76	2.54	2.77	0.81	3.58	4.55	1.57	6.12
Electricity, water, etc.	0.10	0.02	0.11	0.15	0.02	0.17	0.25	0.03	0.28
Construction	3.75	0.51	4.26	1.47	0.14	1.60	5.22	0.64	5.86
Trade, hotel & restaurant	2.39	0.36	2.75	3.19	0.46	3.64	5.57	0.82	6.39
Transport, storage & communication	1.32	0.02	1.33	1.54	0.12	1.66	2.86	0.14	2.99
Other services	1.95	0.77	2.72	2.82	1.51	4.33	4.77	2.28	7.05
Total							36.97	11.78	48.76
2019–20									
Agriculture	14.10	8.18	22.28	0.67	0.32	0.99	14.77	8.51	23.27
Mining & quarrying	0.08	0.00	0.08	0.07	0.00	0.07	0.14	0.01	0.15
Manufacturing	1.86	0.79	2.65	2.70	0.88	3.59	4.56	1.67	6.24
Electricity, water, etc.	0.13	0.01	0.14	0.19	0.02	0.21	0.31	0.03	0.35
Construction	3.82	0.61	4.42	1.60	0.19	1.79	5.42	0.80	6.22
Trade, hotel & restaurant	2.34	0.40	2.74	3.85	0.88	4.73	6.19	1.28	7.47
Transport, storage & communication	1.37	0.02	1.40	1.61	0.14	1.75	2.99	0.16	3.15
Other services	1.78	0.79	2.57	2.64	1.50	4.13	4.42	2.29	6.71
Total							38.80	14.75	53.55

Source: Estimated using PLFS 2018–19 and 2019–20

Economic Census 1998, 2005 and 2013

The exhaustive economic census of 1998, conducted by the Central Statistics Office (CSO), covered 30.35 million enterprises engaged in different economic activities other than crop production and plantation. It dealt with own-account enterprises (establishments without any hired worker) as well as establishments (an enterprise run by employing at least one hired worker). It covered private profit and non-profit institutions, cooperatives and all economic activities, including dharamshalas and temples. A similar survey was conducted in 2005, covering 41.83 million enterprises.

The salient findings pertaining to the ownership of the enterprises are given in Tables 3.5 and Table 3.6. We find that more than half of all enterprises were owned by SCs, STs and OBCs in rural areas, and ownership stood at around 40 per cent in urban areas. This encompassed manufacturing, construction, trade, hotels and restaurants, transport, finance and business, and other services.

Table 3.5
Social Group of Owners of Enterprises in 1998
(In Percent)

Item	Rural	Urban	Combined
SC	9.0	5.8	7.7
ST	5.2	2.3	4.0
OBC	36.0	29.1	33.1
Total of above	50.2	37.2	44.8

Source: Economic Census, Table 2.6, Central Statistical office, 1998

Table 3.6
Social Groups of Owners of Enterprises in 2005
(In Percent)

	Rural	Urban	Combined
SC	10.00	6.97	8.82
ST	4.60	2.13	3.64
OBC	40.57	34.19	38.08
Total of the above	55.17	43.29	50.54

Source: Economic Census 2005; Table 2.5; All India Report, Central Statistical office

We find that nearly half of all enterprises were owned by SCs, STs and OBCs in 2005. In rural areas, this figure was 55 per cent. This encompassed manufacturing, construction, trade, hotels, restaurants, transport, finance, business and other services.

The enterprise survey also revealed that 80 per cent of these enterprises were found to be self-financing. Much of the funding would have come from informal caste networks. What is required to be debated is the enhancement of credit systems for the enterprises, more so to those owned by SCs, STs and OBCs. In other words, the focus should be on 'Vaishyavization' of large segments of our civil society, instead of creating large numbers of 'proletariat' in the fashion of nineteenth-century models. For that we need to recognize caste as the natural social capital present in our system.

According to the sixth economic census (2013), the most recent one, 58.5 million establishments were found to be in operation. Out of these, 34.8 million establishments (59.48 per cent) were found in rural areas, and nearly 23.7 million establishments (40.52 per cent) were found to be located in urban areas.

An establishment is a unit situated in a single location in which predominantly one kind of economic activity is carried out, such that at least a part of the goods and/or services produced by the unit goes for sale (that is, the entire produce is not for sole consumption).

Out of the total number of establishments, 41.97 million (71.74 per cent) were own-account establishments and the remaining 16.53 million (28.26 per cent) were establishments with at least one hired worker. Own-account establishments grew at the rate of 56.02 per cent, while the growth of establishments with hired workers was 15.11 per cent, since the previous census in 2005. Proprietary firms constituted 89 per cent of the establishments, and their social composition is given in Table 3.7.

Table 3.7
Social Group of Owners of Proprietorship
Enterprises in 2013

Group	Percentage
SC	11.4
ST	5.4
OBC	40.8
Total of above	57.6

Note: *The rural and urban categories are not available for the 2013 census*

Source: *Sixth Economic Census, 2016, Ministry of Statistics and Programme Implementation (http://mospi.nic.in/all-india-report-sixth-economic-census)*

Between 1998 and 2013, we find that the SC, ST and OBC categories increased their share of ownership of enterprises, from 45 per cent to 57 per cent, which seems to indicate their increasing political clout as well.

Religion and Sex-Wise Data

The economic census of 2013 also provides religion and sex-wise data of establishment ownership. According to the data, 73.70 per cent of the establishments were owned by Hindus, 13.8 per cent by Muslims, 2.60 per cent by Christians and the rest (9.90 per cent) by the followers of other religions.

Out of the total establishments under women entrepreneurs, the percentage share of various social and religious groups was as follows: OBC: 40.6 per cent; SC: 12.18 per cent; ST: 6.97 per cent; and others: 40.25 per cent; Hindus: 65.6 per cent; Muslims: 12.84 per cent; and Christians: 5.2 per cent. This we will take up as part of social capital at a later stage.

There has been some demand for reservation in private-sector jobs. The share of the private organized sector in GDP as well as in employment is meagre. It may not be more than 15 per cent in either case.[5]

More than employment, the ownership of businesses is important for the SC, ST and OBC communities. We find that more than 50 per cent of enterprises (own account as well as labour employing) are owned by SCs, STs and OBCs, and these small and medium entrepreneurs are the major driving force of the Indian economy. There is a need to provide adequate and timely credit to them from institutional finance and reduce corruption in dealing with the government. This we will discuss later.

4

Caste Categories and Entrepreneurs:

The Unincorporated Sector

The Social Groups of Owners

The survey of unincorporated non-agricultural (excluding construction), proprietary and partnership enterprises conducted by the National Sample Survey Organisation (73rd round), between July 2015 and June 2016, provides interesting insights about the caste composition of the owners of different kinds of enterprises. This was a fairly exhaustive survey and may be repeated in future rounds in this decade.

Information on the social group of the owner or major partner of unincorporated non-agricultural enterprises, operating on the proprietary and partnership basis, was collected during this survey. About 66 per cent of unincorporated non-agricultural proprietary/partnership enterprises were owned by persons belonging to the three backward sections (STs, SCs and OBCs). This proportion was 69 per cent in the case of own-account enterprises (OAEs) and 52 per cent for establishments. Furthermore, nearly 74 per cent of the proprietary/partnership enterprises in rural areas and 59 per cent of those in the urban areas were owned by persons belonging to the three socially backward sections. The details are presented in Table 4.1.

Table 4.2 shows that persons belonging to socially backward sections together owned about 71 per cent of manufacturing enterprises, which were run as either proprietary or on a partnership basis. This proportion was 73 per cent for OAEs and 57 per cent for establishments. About 75 per cent of the enterprises in rural areas and 65 per cent of the enterprises in urban areas were run by socially backward sections. Table 4.3 shows that among the trading enterprises which were run on proprietary or partnership basis, about 62 per cent were owned by persons belonging to the SCs, STs and OBCs. This proportion was 65 per cent for trading OAEs and 43 per cent for trading establishments at an all-India level. The proportion of proprietary and partnership trading enterprises owned by the backward sections was about 72 per cent in rural areas and 53 per cent in urban areas.

The percentage distribution for 'other services' proprietary and partnership enterprises on the basis of the social group of their owner/major partner is given in Table 4.4. About 67 per cent of these enterprises were owned by persons belonging to the STs, SCs and OBCs.

Table 4.1

Percentage Distribution of Proprietary and Partnership Enterprises by the Social Group of Their Owner/Major Partner for Each Sector and Enterprise Type (All India)

Social group of owner/ major partner	PERCENTAGE OF ENTERPRISES								
	Rural			Urban			Rural & Urban		
	OAE	Establishment (Estt)	All	OAE	Estt	All	OAE	Estt	All
(1)	(2)	(3)	(4)	(5)	(6)	(7)	(8)	(9)	(10)
Scheduled tribes	6.9	4.8	6.7	1.6	0.9	1.4	4.5	2.0	4.1
Scheduled castes	16.0	8.7	15.4	11.0	4.2	9.4	13.8	5.5	12.4
Other backward classes	51.7	50.0	51.6	49.4	42.4	47.8	50.7	44.5	49.7
Others	24.6	35.7	25.6	37.2	51.3	40.5	30.3	47.0	32.9
Not known	0.7	0.7	0.7	0.8	1.2	0.9	0.7	1.1	0.8
All India	100.0	100.0	100.0	100.0	100.0	100.0	100.0	100.0	100.0

Source: Operational Characteristics of Unincorporated Non-Agricultural Enterprises (Excluding Construction) in India; NSS 73rd ROUND (July 2015–June 2016) NSS Report No: 581 Statement 15.0 p. 68, Government of India (http://mospi.nic.in/sites/default/files/publication_reports/NSS_581.pdf)

Table 4.2

Percentage Distribution of Proprietary and Partnership Manufacturing Enterprises by Social Group of Their Owner/Major Partner for Each Sector and Enterprise Type (All India)

Social group of owner/ major partner	PERCENTAGE OF ENTERPRISES								
	Rural			Urban			Rural + Urban		
	OAE	Estt	All	OAE	Estt	All	OAE	Estt	All
(1)	(2)	(3)	(4)	(5)	(6)	(7)	(8)	(9)	(10)
Scheduled tribes	6.9	4.5	6.7	1.4	0.9	1.3	4.8	2.1	4.4
Scheduled castes	16.7	9.1	16.1	10.6	5.5	9.4	14.4	6.6	13.3
Other backward classes	52.2	51.7	52.2	57.0	47.2	54.7	54.0	48.7	53.2
Others	23.5	34.1	24.4	30.3	45.5	33.8	26.1	41.8	28.3
Not known	0.7	0.6	0.7	0.8	0.9	0.8	0.7	0.8	0.7
All India	100.0	100.0	100.0	100.0	100.0	100.0	100.0	100.0	100.0

Source: Operational Characteristics of Unincorporated Non-Agricultural Enterprises (Excluding Construction) in India; NSS 73rd ROUND (July 2015–June 2016) NSS Report No: 581 Statement 15.0 p. 69, Government of India (http://mospi.nic.in\sites\default\files\publication_reports\NSS_581.pdf)

Table 4.3

Percentage Distribution of Propriety and Partnership Trading Enterprises by Social Group of Their Owner/Major Partner for Each Sector and Enterprise Type (All India)

Social group of owner/ major partner	PERCENTAGE OF ENTERPRISES									
	Rural			Urban			Rural + Urban		
	OAE	Estt	All	OAE	Estt	All	OAE	Estt	All
(1)	(2)	(3)	(4)	(5)	(6)	(7)	(8)	(9)	(10)
Scheduled tribes	8.3	3.3	8.0	1.6	0.6	1.3	5.1	1.2	4.5
Scheduled castes	13.9	5.2	13.4	9.8	2.8	8.2	12.0	3.3	10.6
Other backward classes	50.6	47.0	50.3	44.8	37.1	43.0	47.8	39.0	46.5
Others	26.4	43.3	27.5	42.9	58.2	46.5	34.3	55.4	37.5
Not known	0.8	1.1	0.8	0.9	1.2	1.0	0.8	1.2	0.9
All India	100.0	100.0	100.0	100.0	100.0	100.0	100.0	100.0	100.0

Source: Operational Characteristics of Unincorporated Non-Agricultural Enterprises (Excluding Construction) in India; NSS 73rd ROUND (July 2015–June 2016) NSS Report No: 581 Statement 15.0 p. 69, Government of India (http://mospi.nic.in/sites/default/files/publication_reports/NSS_581.pdf)

Table 4.4

Percentage Distribution of Propriety and Partnership of Other Services Enterprises by Social Group of Their Owner/Major Partner for Each Sector and Enterprise Type (All India)

Social group of owner/ major partner	PERCENTAGE OF ENTERPRISES								
	Rural			Urban			Rural + Urban		
	OAE	Estt	All	OAE	Estt	All	OAE	Estt	All
(1)	(2)	(3)	(4)	(5)	(6)	(7)	(8)	(9)	(10)
Scheduled tribes	5.0	5.9	5.1	1.7	1.3	1.6	3.4	2.8	3.3
Scheduled castes	17.7	10.6	16.8	12.9	4.9	11.0	15.3	6.7	13.8
Other backward classes	52.6	50.3	52.3	48.9	44.9	48.0	50.8	46.7	50.0
Others	23.9	32.5	25.0	35.9	47.6	38.6	29.9	42.7	32.2
Not known	0.7	0.7	0.7	0.6	1.3	0.8	0.7	1.1	0.8
All India	100.0	100.0	100.0	100.0	100.0	100.0	100.0	100.0	100.0

Source: Operational Characteristics of Unincorporated Non-Agricultural Enterprises (Excluding Construction) in India; NSS 73rd ROUND (July 2015–June 2016) NSS Report No: 581 Statement 15.0 p. 70, Government of India (http://mospi.nic.in/sites/default/files/publication_reports/NSS_581.pdf)

Table 4.5

Percentage Distribution of Proprietary and Partnership Enterprises by Social Group of Their Owner/Major Partner for Each Broad Activity Category and Type of Enterprises (All India)

Social group of owner/ major partner	PERCENTAGE OF ENTERPRISES									
	Manufacturing			Trading			Other services		
	OAE	Estt	All	OAE	Estt	All	OAE	Estt	All
(1)	(2)	(3)	(4)	(5)	(6)	(7)	(8)	(9)	(10)
Scheduled tribes	4.8	2.1	4.4	5.1	1.2	4.5	3.4	2.8	3.3
Scheduled castes	14.4	6.6	13.3	12.0	3.3	10.6	15.3	6.7	13.8
Other backward classes	54.0	48.7	53.2	47.8	39.0	46.5	50.8	46.7	50.0
Others	26.1	41.8	28.3	34.3	55.4	37.5	29.9	42.7	32.2
Not known	0.7	0.8	0.7	0.8	1.2	0.9	0.7	1.1	0.8
All India	100.0	100.0	100.0	100.0	100.0	100.0	100.0	100.0	100.0

Source: Operational Characteristics of Unincorporated Non-Agricultural Enterprises (Excluding Construction) in India; NSS 73rd ROUND (July 2015–June 2016) NSS Report No: 581 Statement 15.0 p. 70, Government of India (http://mospi.nic.in/sites/default/ files/publication_reports/NSS_581.pdf)

This proportion was 69 per cent for OAEs and 56 per cent for establishments. Furthermore, 74 per cent of other services proprietary and partnership enterprises in rural areas and 61 per cent of those in urban areas were run by persons belonging to these socially backward sections.

Table 4.5 presents a comparative picture of the percentage distribution of proprietary and partnership enterprises on the basis of the social group of their owner or major partner for each broad activity category and type of enterprise. The OBCs owned nearly half of the proprietary and partnership enterprises across all activity categories and enterprise types, except for the establishments in trading, where nearly 55 per cent were owned by the social group 'Others'. Among the social groups, the ownership share was the least for STs, at less than 5 per cent across enterprise types and broad activity categories, followed by SCs. The ownership share of the social group 'Others' among establishments was higher than their ownership share among OAEs in each of the three broad activity categories. Whereas in the other three socially backward sections, the ownership shares in OAEs were higher than that in establishments across activity categories.

Chart 4.1
Percentage Distribution of Proprietary and Partnership of Manufacturing Enterprises by Social Group of Their Owner/Partner in India

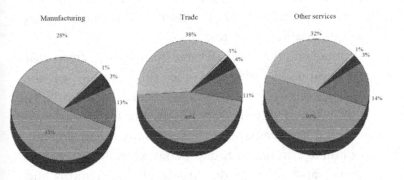

Manufacturing   Trade   Other services

Source: Operational Characteristics of Unincorporated Non-Agricultural Enterprises (Excluding Construction) in India; NSS 73rd ROUND (July 2015 –June 2016) NSS Report No: 581 Statement 15.0 p. 71, Government of India (http://mospi.nic.in/sites/default/files/publication_reports/NSS_581.pdf)

We find from Chart 4.1 that the OBCs constitute the largest segment of proprietors and partners in all categories, namely, manufacturing, trade and other services. Actually, in manufacturing and other services they account for more than 50 per cent. If we add the SC, ST and OBC category, then together they constitute 71 per cent, 62 per cent and 67 per cent in the three categories, respectively. This reveals that 'Vaishyavization' is taking place in our economy across all caste categories, which is similar to the

'Sanskritization' process[1] theorized by M.N. Srinivas from a cultural point of view.

Of course, there are inter-state variations in terms of industry focus among these social segments, which also require a closer study to encourage and further enhance entrepreneurial activities by these social groups in different states.

Incidentally, one of the arguments given for reservations is regarding the enhancement of the 'social status' of these segments. Social backwardness, it is pointed out, is a valid reason for caste-based reservations compared to reservations based on, say, economic criteria. In today's context, politics, cricket, cinema and TV provide substantial social status and hence, maybe the demand should be in these areas, over jobs that entail corporate keyboard punching!

The Marxist postulate is that it is 'inevitable' that the 'petite bourgeoisie' will become a proletariat in the process of the growth of capitalism. The corporate globalizer, who belongs to the metropolitan elite, also argues about 'scale efficiency' and 'modernization', and feels that the 'rational route' is for all these small Vaishyas to disappear and become blue- or white-collar workers for the cause of 'global efficiency'. Both the theories are based on nineteenth-century experiences.

Policy planners and experts need to work on a road map to calibrate changes in our current context. Already, we find that it is difficult to locate a tailor or a cobbler in many towns. Let us remember that Walmart was built in rural America by liquidating thousands of mom-and-pop stores, which are equivalent to our street-corner *kirana* shops.

The arrival of the Internet and cell phones present opportunities to innovate in the linking of millions of small Vaishyas to create scale economies. Indian civilization, over the centuries, has always been innovative and creative in finding solutions to social problems. Maybe the time has come for the government to perform mainly the task of a Kshatriya (internal and external security) and encourage large segments of our society to become Vaishyas through instrumentalities of credit delivery, taxation, social security and development of regional and community-based clusters. This may go a long way in enhancing the social status of the SCs, STs and OBCs, rather than providing some limited job opportunities in listed companies.

5

Social Capital

While the concept of social capital has become fashionable only fairly recently, the term has been in use for more than a century, and its ideas probably go back even further still. The term 'social capital' probably first appeared in the 1916 book *The Rural School Community Center*, published in the United States, that discussed how neighbours could work together to oversee schools.

The author of this work, Lyda Hanifan (1879–1932), who was the supervisor of rural schools in West Virginia, referred to social capital as 'those tangible assets [that] count for most in the daily lives of people: namely goodwill, fellowship, sympathy, and social intercourse among the individuals and families who make up a social unit'.[1]

It is difficult to come up with a single definition of social capital that is acceptable to all sociologists. In a sense it consists of the shared values, links and world view in society, which helps individuals in groups to trust each other and work together.

The Organization for Economic Co-operation and Development (OECD) defines social capital as 'networks together with shared norms, values and understandings that facilitate co-operation within or among groups'. In this definition, networks can be thought of as real-world links between groups or individuals—for instance, networks of friends, family members, networks of co-workers and so on. One thing that bears remembering is that often, our shared norms, values and understanding are not as concrete as our social networks. Sociologists sometimes speak of norms as society's unspoken and largely unquestioned rules, which may not become readily apparent until they are broken. When adults attack a child, for instance, they breach the norms that protect children from harm. Values are often more open to questioning, so much so that societies often debate whether their values are changing. Still, values—such as respect for people's safety and security—are essential in every social group. Put together, these networks and understandings create trust and, thus, enable people to work together.[2]

While there has been much debate over the various forms that social capital takes, one fairly straightforward approach divides it into three main categories:

1. Bonds: Links to people based on a sense of common identity ('people like us')—such as family, close friends and people who share our culture or ethnicity.
2. Bridges: Links that go beyond a shared sense of identity. For instance, distant friends, colleagues and associates.
3. Linkages: Links to people or groups further up or lower down the social ladder.

The potential benefits of social capital can be understood by looking closely at social bonds. Friends and families can help us in lots of ways—emotionally, socially and economically. In the United Kingdom, for example, a government survey found that more people secure jobs through personal contacts than through advertisements. Such support can be even more important in countries where the rule of law is weak or where the state offers few social services: clans can fund the education of relatives and find them work, and also look after orphans and the elderly.

Sociologists like Robert D. Putnam have demonstrated that enormous economic benefits flow from social capital. Contrasting the huge economic success of northern Italy with the relative failure of the southern part, he found that in southern Italy, the mafia had eroded social capital and hence stalled economic development. High levels of trust greatly reduce risks and costs, and thus encourage enterprises and innovation while reducing the costs of redress.

This implies that within groups, financially assisting each other becomes simpler in terms of lending as well as securing capital for new businesses. So social capital ultimately translates into financial capital.[3]

Gurcharan Das, the corporate chief-turned-author and analyst says, 'In the nineteenth century, British colonialists used to blame our caste system for everything wrong in India. Now I have a different perspective. Instead of morally judging caste, I seek to understand its impact on competitiveness. I have come to believe that being endowed with commercial castes is a source of advantage in the global economy.' Joel Kotkin demonstrates these strengths when talking about the case of Palanpur Jains, who have used their caste and family networks in wresting half the global market for uncut diamonds from the Jews.[4]

It is important to understand that the shared sense of community and trust that the Indian commercial castes, like the Marwaris, Jains, Bohras, Chettiars and others, have traditionally demonstrated has acted as a major social capital for them.

Sociologists underline that a nation could be maintained successfully only when people are able to live with each other in groups. The French sociologist Émile Durkheim had earlier noted, 'A nation can be maintained only if between the state and the individual there is interposed a whole series of secondary groups . . . community orientation creates trust among the members of the society.'[5]

Francis Fukuyama notes that trust has an economic value. He says, 'The ability to associate depends, in turn on the degree to which communities share norms and values and are able to subordinate individual interests to those of larger groups . . . trust results in social capital.'[6]

Swaminathan Aiyar defines social capital in the following way: 'Unlike financial or human capital it cannot be owned by individuals, only by social groups. This defines social capital. Being less tangible than financial or human capital it is difficult to measure and so has been ignored in the past. Yet it is an invaluable asset.'[7]

In his 2000 book, *Bowling Alone: The Collapse and Revival of American Community*, Robert Putnam argued that while Americans had become wealthier, their sense of community had withered. He felt that cities and traditional suburbs had given way to 'edge cities' and 'exurbs', which were vast, anonymous places where people only slept and worked and did little else. Increasingly, people spent more and more time in the office, in commuting to work and in watching TV alone, and, therefore, had little time for joining community groups, voluntary organizations, and socializing with neighbours, friends and even family. A demonstration of this decline was in the way, Putnam believed, Americans played ten-pin bowling, a popular American sport. He found that although bowling was still extremely popular, Americans were no longer competing against each other in the once-popular local leagues. Instead, more often than not they were bowling alone. This decline of the community networks that once led Americans to bowl together, to Putnam, represented a loss of social capital.[8]

The concept of social capital also has its critics. One arguments states that bonds can hinder people, too. Since tightly knit communities, such as some immigrant groups, often have strong social bonds and individuals rely heavily on relatives or people of the same ethnic background for support, the lack of social bridges might keep them as eternal outsiders from society and hinder their economic progress. Of course, tightly knit groups may exclude themselves too, but they may also be excluded by the wider community. Without 'bridging' social capital, 'bonding' groups can become isolated and disenfranchised from the rest of society and, most importantly, from groups with which bridging must occur in order to denote an 'increase' in social capital. Bonding social capital is a necessary antecedent for the development of the more powerful form of bridging social capital.[9]

Another argument that's been made is that Putnam got it wrong when he said social engagement is eroding. Instead, it may just be evolving. Rather than joining groups in our neighbourhoods, like bowling leagues, we're now joining groups made up of people who share our beliefs—on fighting for the environment, gay rights, etc.

These groups—such as a branch of Greenpeace or Amnesty International—may exist in the 'real' world, but they may also exist only virtually on the Internet, which is arguably creating whole new 'communities' of people who may never physically meet but who share common values and interests.

Not everyone, however, is convinced that these new forms of community have the same value as the more traditional forms.

The Indian Scenario

Perhaps, more than the ten-pin bowling alley, the local church was a better representation of social capital in the USA till the middle of the last century. The church played an important role in the local community and also facilitated the development of a vast network.

In Hinduism, there is no organized church as in Western countries, where people congregate every week. But there are well-defined social groups in the form of castes. They have common bonds through marriage and fraternal relationships, besides having commonalities pertaining to birth, marriage and death ceremonies that are part of their *samskaras* (rituals).

Caste and Its Complexities

1. Defining caste: Defining a caste is not very easy, except to safely say that a caste has many commonalities in ceremonies at the time of birth, marriage and death. It also has commonalities in food habits and, in some cases, even in sartorial

habits. The actual number of castes is not definitely known. Some popular literature speaks of as many as 3000 major castes and around 22,000 sub-castes.

2. Caste hierarchy: Then there is the subject of caste hierarchy. The basic issue here is the assumption that there exists one caste system when we actually have many caste systems. The English notions of class and class hierarchy have been used in trying to identify one caste system and a hierarchy thereof. It is also assumed that caste is a rigid system that is both hierarchical and oppressive. But as the renowned sociologist Dipankar Gupta wrote, 'In fact, it is more realistic to say that there are probably as many hierarchies as there are castes in India. To believe that there is a single caste order to which every caste, from Brahmin to untouchable, acquiesce ideologically, is a gross misreading of facts on the ground.' The truth is that no caste, howsoever lowly placed it may be, accepts social status as the reason for its degradation. The so-called lower castes often claim that they were once ruling castes, and due to defeat in wars or other social upheavals they have been categorized as lower and not due to birth.

3. Caste malleability: Another issue is that the idea of caste has been very malleable. For instance, due to electoral politics many sub-castes try to identify themselves with a single aggregated caste. For instance, as discussed earlier, there are three major

sub-castes among the Thevars in Tamil Nadu. They are hence known as 'Mukkulothor' (people with three *kulams* or clans). But in the last thirty years or so they have all identified themselves as Thevars, and this has helped the caste consolidate in the context of electoral politics.[10]

4. Caste aggregation: In 2018, as indicated earlier, when the Karnataka government wanted to declare the Lingayat community as a separate religion, it emerged that they had some ninety-seven sub-categories within that broad nomenclature. Similar examples can be given for other parts of the country also. We can term it as the era of aggregation and not fragmentation. In the nineteenth and the early part of the twentieth centuries, we find more and more finer divisions of a caste, most of them being endogamous. But post Independence, we find more aggregation, since it helps in electoral politics, where numbers matter.

5. Enumerating caste: The British did initially try to enumerate caste groups as well as understand the hierarchy of castes through census. But when census returns proved to be much more complex, differentiated and not compatible regionally, these and similar ideas of sub-categorization were gradually abandoned. The British ceased their efforts to establish a hierarchical order of castes after 1901 and stopped counting castes altogether after 1931.[11] The Census of 2011 attempted to enumerate castes but ended up with a huge

problem. The census enumerators who covered 330 million households ended up with a list of 4.6 million entries, which implied that, on an average, only seventy-two households used the same phrase to identify their caste.[12]

Understanding the Social–Capital Role of Caste

Caste is decided at birth, even though it is argued, as we will see elsewhere, that jati and varna are different and varna is actually decided by one's vocation. But we will stick to the contemporary idea of caste based on birth, even though you can technically be outside your caste—meaning not following the customs and rituals of the caste—of your own volition and particularly if you are in major cities, where this is much easier.

But caste acts as a network, providing you access to information on emerging opportunities. It can also provide credit for business and acts as a facilitator of risk management. In a sense, it helps mitigate failures and encourages a person to innovate.

In the case of traditional white-collar castes, it provides access to information on new areas of study to help in job opportunities. This could come from extended family networks and, in the current context, even the Internet. You find that there are educational and job opportunities from caste and sub-caste members who belong to the extended family. It is interesting that there are many social groups on the Internet based on caste, and most of them discuss education, jobs, matrimony and rituals. Some also discuss new start-ups and business opportunities.

Another example is the network of electrical appliance stores established in Bengaluru by Mewaris from Rajasthan, indicating a significant exchange of information and support in initial financing and market access. They often utilize their caste network for sourcing materials for their retail business.

Our focus is more on the aggregated or broad caste categories as they exist today rather than the sub-caste discussion. We focus on caste as it exists today to highlight the economic benefits arising out of its role.

6

Social Capital and Entrepreneurship

In discussions on social capital, the importance of social capital in entrepreneurship has not been discussed sufficiently. Most Western sociologists consider social capital as more important in relationships and social cooperation, though a few of them do underline the importance of social capital from the point of view of credit, capital and mutual support.

As already referred to in Chapter 5, Emile Durkheim, in one of his earlier works, *The Division of Labour in Society* (originally published in 1897), says, 'A nation can be maintained only if, between the State and the individual, there is interposed a whole series of secondary groups near enough to the individuals to attract them strongly in their sphere of action and drag them, in this way, into the general torrent of social life . . . Occupational groups are suited to fill this role, and that is their destiny . . .'

Francis Fukuyama, in his celebrated work *Trust*, published in 1995, stresses the point that, 'The ability to associate depends . . . on the degree to which communities share norms and values . . . Out of such shared values comes trust, and trust has a large and measurable economic value.'

In his work, Fukuyama examines a wide range of national cultures in order to better understand the underlying principles that result in social and economic prosperity. His contention is that we cannot divorce economic life from cultural life and that in an era when social capital is as important as physical capital, only those societies with a high degree of social trust will be able to create the flexible, large-scale business organizations that are needed to compete in the new global economy.

Arguing against what he sees as the increasing drift of American culture into extreme forms of individualism, Fukuyama examines the interconnectedness of economic life with cultural life and argues that extreme individualism could have dire consequences for the nation's economic health.

Hence, we can say that social capital has an important role to play in economic activities and acts as a catalyst for entrepreneurship. Basically, Fukuyama argues that social trust emanates from social capital, which facilitates entrepreneurship within the group. It is seen among the Mormons and among various other church groups, like the Roman Catholics, Presbyterians, Episcopalians, Baptists and other older denominations.

The business activities of the Mormons—for instance, the Marriot group of hotels—highlight the closely knit ownership and funding that one notices among such groups and among other groups belonging to other denominations that started many business enterprises in the middle of the twentieth century.

In the past, the social group was geography-specific, but that is not true any more. This aspect is examined in greater detail in later chapters.

Social capital is useful in developing and sustaining entrepreneurship in the following ways:

- **Provision of initial capital:** This is an important aspect, particularly in a developing economy like India. A substantial portion of financing for enterprises in small and medium sectors comes from family and community. We find that in India around 90 per cent of the financing of enterprises takes place through own sources, namely self, family, extended family and community. We have data for the economic census of 2005 as well as of 2013, undertaken by the Central Statistics Office (CSO). In 2005, the census found that out of 41.8 million enterprises, more than 95 per cent were financed by family and community. Another survey of 58 million non-agricultural unincorporated enterprises in the sixty-seventh survey of the National Sample Survey Office (NSSO), conducted in 2009–10, showed that more than 95 per cent of them were financed by non-institutional finance, that is, the family or community. As per the economic census of 2013, 58.5 million establishments were found to be in operation, out of which 34.8 million establishments (59.48 per cent) were found in rural areas and nearly 23.7 million establishments (40.52 per cent) were found to be located in urban areas. Among these establishments, 45.37 million (77.55 per cent) were engaged in non-agricultural activities, while the remaining 13.13 million (22.45 per cent) were engaged in agricultural activities other than crop production and plantation. 41.97 million (71.74 per cent) of these were own-account establishments and the remaining 16.53 million (28.26 per cent) were establishments with at least one hired worker. Own-account establishments grew at the rate of 56.02 per cent, while the growth of establishments with hired workers was 15.11 per cent (since 2005). About 30.13 million (71.81 per cent) of the total 41.96 million own-account establishments were found engaged in non-agricultural activities, whereas around 11.83 million (28.19 per cent) were engaged in agricultural activities.

- **Major source of finance:** A total of 11.37 million agricultural establishments were self-financed, with a concentration of 91.89 per cent in rural areas. In rural India, 86.5 per cent of the agricultural establishments were self-financed, whereas this figure was 88.2 per cent for urban India. Self-finance includes funding from family, extended family and caste sources.[1]

- **Donations/transfers from other agencies:** Mainly consisting of benefits from extended family members and others during occasions like marriage, childbirth, etc., this was the next major source of finance, with a share of 9 per cent. Financial assistance from government sources and borrowing from financial institutions as a major source of finance were 2.1 per cent and 1.1 per cent, respectively, at the all-India level. There were 45.36 million non-agricultural establishments (22.71 million in rural areas and 22.65 million in urban areas) in the country, which accounted for 77.55 per cent of the total establishments. Out of these, 30.13 million (66.43 per cent) were own-account establishments and the remaining, about 15.23 million (33.57 per cent), were establishments with at least one hired worker. A total of 35.48 million (78.2 per cent) non-agricultural establishments were self-financed, with a concentration of 53.44 per cent in urban areas. In rural India, 72.7 per cent of the non-agricultural establishments were self-financed, whereas this figure was 83.7 per cent in urban India. Donations/transfers from other agencies and financial assistance from government sources were the next two major sources of finance, reported as supporting 11.2 per cent and 6.9 per cent of the establishments, respectively.
- **Assistance to women entrepreneurs:** The 2013 economic census also collected data on women entrepreneurs. The total number of establishments

owned by women entrepreneurs was 8 million, out of which 5.2 million, constituting about 65.12 per cent of the total establishments, were located in rural areas, while the remaining 2.8 million (34.88 per cent) were located in urban areas. Almost 79 per cent of these women-run establishments were self-financed.

Based on these exhaustive surveys, we find that family and caste play a major role in the financing of the entrepreneurs belonging to micro, small and medium enterprises. This is true of women entrepreneurs as well. During our survey of entrepreneurs in clusters across India, which has been discussed in detail in Chapter 7, we found that caste affiliations do help in acquiring finances to start a business as well as towards running it. This approach has relatively less paperwork, and credit rating is acquired through informal methods. The fact that the community is there to encourage repayment makes the transaction much easier. The presence of social capital reinforces that it is a relationship-oriented economy rather than contract- or rule-oriented. In all financial transactions based on relationships and trust, the role of social capital is critical.

Caste as social capital facilitates the following in the running of a business:

- **Market access:** Social capital facilitates access to new markets. The existing entrepreneur encourages individuals within his extended family or caste to explore new markets where he may not be interested in growing. Market information and clues regarding the nature of customers and trends are given free of cost, where it is otherwise provided by modern market research agencies at a price. For instance, in the Tiruppur textile market, many new foreign markets were introduced to newcomers, and they were encouraged to develop there. In local restaurant and retail trade businesses we observe a similar trend. Often, labour for such establishments is drawn from the entrepreneur's own caste, from his or her village or district, when new units are being set up. Sometimes, these people might go on to establish future establishments of their own. In that sense, it is nothing but the training of future entrepreneurs.

- **Intricacies of local laws/regulations and avoidance:** When a person starts a new business, perhaps a retail shop or a restaurant, either in the US or in an Indian city, he needs to understand the intricacies of several laws and regulations pertaining to operations, taxation, markets and so on. By tapping into caste networks, he has an advantage in terms of his social capital, in getting to know the dos and don'ts of business. Sometimes, the local regulations and dealing with the regulators could include tricky matters relating to bribery and other kinds of rent-seeking. How to negotiate these matters is an area of business that is not taught even in business schools but can be understood informally.

- **Availability of loyal labour:** In human resource groups, there is a popular saying that people should be recruited for their attitude as skills can always be imparted. As previously stated, in many businesses we find that labour is brought in from the entrepreneur's own district or village, be it in retail, hospitality or transport. Unless it is a very special type of skilled labour, the practice is to hire from one's own caste and extended community. For instance, a substantial portion of the electrical retail trade in Bengaluru is run by people from Rajasthan, mostly people from the Mewar region. Their assistants and helpers are also from the same region and often belong to the extended family or the same caste. Many a time, these assistants set up their own shops in newly developing areas using the skills they have learnt working in the shops of their caste brethren. In the case of skilled labour too, the spread of information and community linkages are important. In many parts of the country, a good number of plumbers are from Kendrapara in Odisha. Clearly, the social capital of caste and community facilitates mobility to urban areas and access to new markets.

- **Availability of credit:** Around 60 per cent of the credit needs of our economy are met by non-bank sources.[2] The economic census data quoted above reinforces our conclusion. Actually, it even suggests that our figure may be conservative. In any case, it is easier to get credit from chits, moneylenders, *kuri* and other sources from within the community. Credit is sourced much faster and with less paperwork, with gold often used as collateral. The assurance of other members of the community, though informal, makes it easier to provide credit, since social pressure will work when it comes to recovery. In their pioneering study on household repayment behaviour, *The Role of Social Capital, Institutional, Political, and Religious Beliefs*, Dimitris Georgarakos and Sven Fürth highlight the importance of social capital in repayment behaviour. They state the following: 'We examine the influence of social capital, beliefs about corruption, public perceptions about the justice system, religiosity, and political views, on household repayment behaviour after taking into account household-specific and legal or institutional factors that existing literature has identified as important. We find that households living in regions with more dense beliefs about corruption in the country or in authorities that have an immediate power of execution (police) are more likely to delay or skip scheduled payments. We also show that arrears are more common in regions where more people find it difficult to win a dispute with a bank, political views are more left-wing, and people are less religious. Furthermore, we show that high stocks of social capital induce good repayment behaviour, net of the influence of informal borrowing, of beliefs about corruption and the legal environment, of religiosity, of economic growth, and of social stigma considerations related to the observed repayment behaviour of other households in the region. This remaining effect can be consistent with the fact that households in high social capital communities have strong ethical considerations and face a higher hazard of losing their standing in the group and access to the positive externalities of social capital.'[3] In our survey elaborated in Chapter 7, we found in many locations that the 'non-repayment' of borrowings was considered as greatly impacting family and self-respect. It was an issue not linked to law but to God. It was also an issue of *izzat* (honour). So lending and borrowing is facilitated by social capital since there is an unsaid guarantee provided by the community.

- **Acceptance of failure:** Social capital not only provides funding for new ventures but also helps in creating a climate where failures are not looked down upon. Actually, many times the extended family or community act as risk mitigators and encourage youngsters to not lose heart. They could provide easy terms of repayment and also facilitate the setting up of new businesses. In that sense, community leaders act as friends, philosophers and guides, and treat business failures as a normal possibility.

Having considered the above parameters regarding social capital acting as a facilitator in entrepreneurship, we will now explore the Indian scenario by studying different economic clusters to elaborate on the role of caste as social capital.

7

Caste and Economic Clusters

Clusters occupy a significant place in the economic scenario in India and play a crucial role in the development of the Indian businesses. Their contributions to national income, employment, exports and innovation are very significant. The United Nations Industrial Development Organization (UNIDO) has estimated the presence of approximately 350 small-scale industrial clusters and around 2000 rural- and artisan-based clusters in the country, contributing about 60 per cent of the manufacturing done for exports and about 40 per cent of the employment in the manufacturing industry. The Ministry of Micro, Small and Medium Enterprises, Government of India, has estimated that there are 2042 clusters of which 1223 are in the registered sector in twenty-six states, and another 819 in the unregistered sectors in twenty-five states and union territories.[1]

Clusters can be defined as sectoral and geographical concentration of enterprises, particularly in the small and medium enterprises (SME) sector. Faced with common opportunities and threats, these clusters give rise to external economies, for instance, through specialized suppliers of raw materials, components and machinery, sector-specific skills and so on. Clusters also favour the emergence of specialized technical, administrative and financial services, create a conducive ground for the development of inter-firm cooperation and specialization, as well as of cooperation among public and private local institutions to promote local production, innovation and collective learning.[2]

In 2000, a team including chartered accountants, academicians, businessmen and others visited and studied forty-five economic clusters covering ten jatis (communities) engaged in fifty different industries, businesses and services in the states of Tamil Nadu, Gujarat, Punjab, Karnataka and united Andhra Pradesh. The studies were mostly interactive and aimed to understand the functioning of clusters.

We found that most of the clusters specialized in a particular economic activity and were run by specific caste groups. The clusters contributed significantly to output, employment and exports in the different states. Thus, the study of several clusters spread across various regions of the country points to the role of community in emerging entrepreneurial development. Most government-commissioned studies do not stress on the caste and community linkages of clusters, choosing to focus only on economic activities instead.

The organization of industry into homogeneous clusters has been a historical phenomenon. Even for large industries, clusters develop because of the growth of ancillary industries. Being a part of a cluster is important for the sustainable growth of MSMEs. In India, there are around 7000 clusters in traditional handloom, handicrafts and modern SME industry segments (see Table 7.1). In addition to the clusters shown in the table, it is estimated that there are about 2500 unmapped rural industry clusters in the country.

Studies on Clusters

Clusters can also be considered as part of a bigger value-chain mechanism (including raw materials, intermediates, finished products and marketing), where the value chain extends beyond geographically defined boundaries. Defined by relationships rather than a particular product or function, clusters include organizations across multiple traditional industrial classifications, which make drawing the categorical boundaries of a cluster a challenge. Specifically, participants in industry clusters include:

- Organizations providing similar and related goods or services
- Specialized suppliers of goods, services and financial capital (backward linkages)

- Distributors and local customers (forward linkages)
- Companies with complementary products (lateral linkages)

Table 7.1

Distribution of Clusters in India by Regions

	Traditional Manufacturing			Micro Enterprises		
	SME		Handloom	Handicrafts		Total
	No.	%	No.	%	No.	%	
North	315	28.1	124	25.1	627	20.3	1066
East	148	13.2	110	22.2	807	26.2	1065
West	294	26.2	122	24.6	816	26.5	1232
South	350	31.2	83	16.8	537	17.4	970
North-east	15	1.3	56	11.3	297	9.6	368
Total	1122	100	495	100	3084	100	4701

Source: Policy and Status Paper on Cluster Development in India, Foundation for MSME and http://planningcommission.gov.in/ aboutus/committee/wrkgrp12/wg_aggregation.pdf

- Companies employing related skills or technologies or common inputs (lateral linkages)
- Related research, education and training institutions, such as universities
- Community colleges and workforce training programmes

- Cluster support organizations, such as trade and professional associations
- Business councils and standards-setting organizations[3]

Report of the Working Group on Micro, Small and Medium Enterprises Growth for the Twelfth Five-Year Plan (2012–17) identified credit availability and skill development as two important aspects of the development of MSME clusters.[4] Another exhaustive study on SME clusters in India looks at footwear market clusters in Agra and Kolkata and garment-related clusters in Tiruppur. It concludes, 'The horizontal and vertical relations of an industrial cluster rest upon a fine balance between competition and cooperation. Competition and cooperation in a cluster are not substitute modes of interaction. The cluster should continuously create opportunities and environment for fierce competition between firms at the enterprise level while at the same time continuously get exposed to external challenges of competition that facilitate cooperation and joint action between firms in order to access collective indivisible inputs. Hence the vertical relations need not be rigid and the space for competition within suppliers should prevail. The homogenising trend within the cluster—if it increases beyond a critical limit and gets mediated through the disciplining forces of relations and institutions—gradually loses the attributes of flexibility.'[5]

Interestingly, the Bureau of Energy Efficiency of the Ministry of Power has conducted an exhaustive study of thirty-five SME clusters, like the Firozabad glass cluster, the Coimbatore foundry cluster, the Bhimavaram ice plants and so on. But the focus was only on energy efficiency and methods to improve it.[6]

A 2014 research paper in the *Journal of Business Ethics* that looked at the clusters in China, Brazil and India assesses the significance of small-firm clusters as critical sites of industrial competitiveness. It said, 'Some of the most significant examples of successful, innovative and internationally competitive small firm clusters from the developing world are located in the "Rising Powers" and cluster promotion is a core element of national industrial policy in some of these countries.'[7]

Most government studies on clusters do not analyse the caste composition and ownership of clusters. Some of them do talk of the role of the scheduled castes and Muslims in the leather industry, but more as an aside. But we find that caste is primarily responsible for creating clusters. Whether it is Tiruppur in Tamil Nadu (the Gounders), Surat in Gujarat (the Patels), Sivakasi in Tamil Nadu (the Nadars) or Jamnagar in Gujarat (the Jadejas/Patels), what has actually taken place is the development of a cluster mainly by an agricultural caste based on local materials or markets. These clusters began to occupy an important position, since caste support was available for new entrants, labour was available locally and market access was established using political connections.

Major Characteristics of Clusters

The following characteristics are reflective of the caste composition of clusters since they provide cooperation and trust as provided through caste as social capital.

Promoted and Run by Ordinary Persons

Typically, clusters are promoted and run by ordinary persons—most of whom are first-generation entrepreneurs. The initial units in all these clusters were promoted by one or more entrepreneurial people. Later, the number of units grew due to the influence of the promoters of the earlier units and the success of the initial ventures.

Usually, the Original Promoters Had Very Little Formal Education

The Sankagiri transport cluster of Tamil Nadu is the second-largest lorry traffic cluster in the country. More than 80 per cent of this cluster's truck owners used to be drivers and cleaners themselves. Similarly, in the knitwear industry in Tiruppur, more than 90 per cent are from agricultural backgrounds, Gounders by caste. There are studies to show that many Tiruppur entrepreneurs have less than a high-school education but significant shop-floor experience. The descendants of farmers from Palanpur and Kathiawar have created the diamond hub in Surat, which provides employment to large numbers in Antwerp and New York. Here, too, many entrepreneurs have little formal education but plenty of practical knowledge. This experience has been gained in the units run by other family members or community members. Hence, the community becomes crucial for gaining practical knowledge.[8]

Large Appetite for Risk-Taking

Many members of the Tiruppur (knitted garments), Sivakasi (matches), Namakkal (poultry/truck building) Rajkot (engineering), Surat (diamonds) and Jamnagar (brassware) clusters have been found to be risk-takers. They entered businesses about which they did not possess any involved knowledge, but they intuitively understood market opportunities. The people of Saurashtra, for example, severely affected by drought, moved out to cities like Surat in search of jobs, began to work in the diamond industry and ended up dominating it. Interestingly, the failure of agriculture in areas like Tiruppur, Namakkal, Jamnagar and Sivakasi also gave rise to the development of clusters by risk-taking farmers.

Relationship-Based Business and Faith-Based Transactions

Clusters being relatively small places, a sense of fraternity exists in them. Often, most of these clusters are dominated by one or two communities.

The Jamnagar brassware industry is dominated by members of the Patel community, while the Sivakasi fireworks and matches industry is dominated by the Nadars. The transactions within these communities are mostly relationship-based and not written contract-based. This relationship extends beyond clusters and, sometimes, even to foreign countries. Interestingly, even with members of other communities in the cluster, trust-based transactions take place. For instance, Marwaris are present in many of the Tamil Nadu clusters in small numbers and are also involved in these relationship-based transactions. A study of the Dindigul leather cluster revealed the close relationship among entrepreneurs belonging to different religious communities, like Muslims, Jains and Hindus, all of whose transactions were based on relationships and were not rule-based.

Clusters Are Self-Developed

Most of the clusters are self-developed and self-dependent, and not state-dependent. They have been developed by entrepreneurs themselves, through their own initiatives and efforts. For example, around the 1920s, there was a big crop failure around Sivakasi, a dry area in Tamil Nadu. Two visionaries—Ayya Nadar and Shanmugha Nadar—people from very ordinary backgrounds then went to Kolkata to seek employment. There, they learnt the trade of making matches. Eventually, they established their own unit with the financial support given by one Chinna Nadar of Trichy. Today, Sivakasi manufactures 80 per cent of India's safety matches, 90 per cent of fireworks and, in recent times, has become a destination for offset printing solutions, with about 60 per cent of the market share in this segment.

After the initial development of these clusters, governments did step in to provide some infrastructural facilities like power and water. But much of the early initiative was independently organized. Sometimes, clusters also develop others that help to make the cluster a cohesive grouping. Educational institutions and temples facilitate the strengthening of caste bonds, in terms of children studying in those institutions and senior citizens running the temples.

Clusters Are Self-Financed

As stated earlier, entrepreneurs in own-account enterprises as well as establishments employing hired labour are mostly dependent on funding from family and community. In fact, bank financing for the working capital needs of MSMEs has fallen in the last two decades. A study of the Karur cluster in Tamil Nadu (known for bus body building and the manufacture of nylon nets in small industries) showed that out of the estimated funds of Rs 2400 crore in 2001, more than two-thirds came from local financers of the community, even though there were more than fifty branches of banks nearby and the banking headquarters of two nationalized banks were located in Karur.[9] In other words, the dependence of businesses on non-bank sources, particularly the community, are extensive.

Cooperation and Competition

We also observe that within clusters there is competition, but at the same time there is a high level of cooperation. For instance, when some orders cannot be fully met by one unit, then the help of other units is sought and obtained very easily. With reference to developing new markets as well as the adoption of new technology, the same logic applies. What is termed as 'cooperative competition' in modern management jargon is actually practised in these clusters. There are virtually no instances of hostile takeovers. Often, when a unit is not performing well, the tendency is to help the unit since it belongs to a member of the extended community.

That caste has played an important role in the development of clusters is recognized by many modern studies. The World Bank suggests that the remarkable growth of Tiruppur is due to the coordinated efforts of the Gounder community. The extent of networking and contract enforcement mechanism available with caste institutions is not fully appreciated. The same is true regarding the Nadar community in Sivakasi. For instance, 'Moi Ezuthuthal' is a form of credit mechanism prevalent among the Nadar community. This is a practice prevalent among the Nadars and other communities in southern Tamil Nadu through which funds are generated for business activities by arranging a community feast.[10]

Clearly, clusters are not anonymous groups of individual entrepreneurs, but interconnected extended families and caste-based communities. This facilitates dealing with failures caused by risk-taking. Actually, there is risk-sharing, and failure is not looked down upon. The extended family or community extends its help in the context of distress and failure, and this acts as a major cushion in undertaking risky activities, like exploring newer markets or innovating new product lines. Thus, clusters act as drivers of economic activities facilitated by family, extended family and caste networks. We will now discuss how various castes have been able to benefit from these clusters in terms of upward mobility.

8

The 'Vaishyavization' of India

In the traditional fourfold caste classification system, a Vaishya is understood to be a businessperson or someone from a farming background. By and large, the role of the Vaishya or, more specifically, the role of the Bania in recent times has been understood in terms of starting and running different kinds of business enterprises. Early post-Independence governments started out with the goal of trying to own the commanding heights of our economy to develop a socialistic pattern of society. This started with the Second Five-Year Plan under the Planning Commission chairman P.C. Mahalanobis. In a sense, it imitated the Soviet model of development. But it did not fully succeed due to a lack of probity in public life on the part of bureaucrats, politicians and executives in these public enterprises. Also, with the fall of the Berlin Wall in 1989 and the collapse of the communist system in Eastern Europe and in the Soviet Union, the socialistic pattern began to be questioned.

The government led by P.V. Narasimha Rao, which came to power in India in 1991, dismantled a substantial portion of the government edifice and encouraged private initiatives. This plan was crafted by the then finance minister, Manmohan Singh, in the early '90s. This unleashed a major thrust towards entrepreneurship. At the same time, the information technology revolution encouraged many first-generation entrepreneurs who came from the traditional 'office-going' category and also motivated many people from farming communities to become entrepreneurs. Suddenly, what used to be dirty words in the Nehru era, namely, 'Bania' and 'profits', became very respectable, and thus started the 'Vaishyavization' of India, where everyone wants to become a Bania. It is similar to the Sanskritization process enunciated by M.N. Srinivas, but in a different form. As previously discussed, several such examples of Vaishyavization exist, some predating the financial reforms of 1991.

The World Bank suggests that the remarkable growth of Tiruppur is due to the coordinated efforts of members of the agricultural Gounder caste, with some members switching from their traditional occupation to entrepreneurship.

Since 1985, Tiruppur has become a hotbed of economic activity in the production of knitted garments. By the 1990s, with high growth rates of exports, Tiruppur became a world leader in the knitted garment industry. The success of this industry is striking. This is particularly so as the production of knitted garments is capital-intensive, and the state banking monopoly had been ineffective at providing capital funds to efficient entrepreneurs, especially at the levels necessary to sustain Tiruppur's high growth rates.

What is behind this story of development? 'The needed capital was raised within the Gounder community, a caste relegated to land-based activities, relying on its community and family network. Those with capital in the Gounder community transferred it to others in the community through long-established informal credit institutions, and rotating savings and credit associations. These networks were viewed as more reliable in transmitting information and enforcing contracts than the banking and legal systems that offered weak protection of creditor rights'[1]

The Nadars of Sivakasi in Tamil Nadu are another example. Derisively called 'Shanars' until about seventy years ago, they have proved themselves in the trade, restaurant, transport, matches and printing sectors, and the whole community has enhanced its position instead of one or two members who might have benefited from reservation in government services.

The Kite-Making Industry of Ahmedabad

While Uttarayan, the mid-January festival during Sankranthi for flying kites, has been a favourite with the Gujaratis since long, it was the Gujarat government which turned it into a major tourism event. Since 1989, Ahmedabad has been hosting the International Kite Festival (IKF). However, it has been significantly scaled up in the last decade, which has also seen significant expansion of commercial activities around it.

The IKF is a major festival in Ahmedabad and in many other towns in Gujarat. The kite-making industry in Gujarat is now worth around Rs 800 crore. Back in 2001–02, the kite industry had a turnover of Rs 35 crore, but by 2013–14, it had grown to Rs 500 crore and had become a source of livelihood for several families. Many members of the Muslim community are involved as entrepreneurs as well as labourers in this business.

Interestingly, Narendra Modi—former chief minister of Gujarat and currently the prime minister of India—was a regular participant at kite festivals. He noticed the poor quality of materials used for making kites and commissioned a survey of kite-making clusters. Then, design institutes were roped in for better designs and value additions in terms of good-quality raw materials. Apart from providing a boost to the kite-making industry, which is now generating much more employment, this move has also led to significant growth in terms of people travelling to Gujarat for events connected with the kite festival, which has now assumed an international scale.

At least 70 per cent of the workers employed in the industry are women belonging to the Muslim community. Many of them live in the Jamalpur area,

which is predominantly Muslim, in Ahmedabad. A
number of people from the Jamalpur area are involved
in kite-making. Also, with the scaling up of the kite
festival, the demand for kites has gone up considerably,
and though it is largely a seasonal activity, kite-making
has become an important source of employment,
sometimes providing enough income to some to sustain
people for the whole year.[2]

Muslims and Scheduled Castes

The leather industry employs about 2.5 million people
and had an annual turnover of more than Rs 32,000
crore in 2016. This industry, too, is deeply embedded
in the social structure of caste and community. Many
people engaged in the industry (entrepreneurs as well as
workers) are, even today, from the traditional leather-
working castes (belonging to the lower castes in the
caste hierarchy) and the Muslim community. Given that
the industry is an ancient one and has deep links with
the social structure, the organizational structure that
has emerged is a very complex one and contains within
it elements of continuity with traditional structures as
well as those that represent a break with them.

Also, the dynamics of the industry have been
shaped, to a large extent, by export orientation from
colonial times. The sector is dominated by small-scale
firms, although there also exist a significant number of
medium- and large-sized firms in all segments of the
industry. The industry is concentrated in several leather

clusters in four or five separate locations across the country, with each cluster containing different kinds of enterprises and organizational structures. The major production centres of leather and leather products are located in Chennai, Ambur, Ranipet, Vaniyambadi, Trichy and Dindigul in Tamil Nadu; Kolkata in West Bengal; Kanpur and Agra in Uttar Pradesh; Jalandhar in Punjab; Delhi; Hyderabad in Telangana; Bangalore in Karnataka and Mumbai in Maharashtra. Tamil Nadu is currently the biggest leather exporter (40 per cent) of the country, and its share in India's total output of leather products is 70 per cent.[3]

In the leather business, Muslims are present in significant numbers as entrepreneurs and sections of the scheduled castes act as labourers. Hindus are averse to dealing with cows, cowhide, etc., since many consider the cow as sacred. Hence their presence in this business is limited. Today, we find that some of the scheduled castes have become entrepreneurs in this business, creating 'Dalit enterprises'.

Caste and the New Capitalists

A vast range of literature is available on the traditional business communities of India, like the Marwaris, Sindhis, Kutchis, Bohras, Patels, and the nature of the global networks some of them have created. In a financial sense, caste has provided the edge for these communities, enabling them to become risk-takers, since failure is recognized and condoned and sometimes even encouraged by the group. This has resulted in the creation of entrepreneurial communities instead of a large number of proletariats in the fashion of nineteenth-century models. Given this fact, we need to recognize caste as the natural social capital present in our system.

In his pioneering work on new capitalists and caste, Harish Damodaran elaborates on the emerging trends of new businesses and their relation to caste. He delineates three general trajectories of industrial transition by communities:

- The first is the conventional bazaar-to-factory route involving the various Bania and Vaishya groups.
- The second, which he identifies as the 'from office-to-factory' route, refers to the Brahmins, Khatris, Kayasthas, the Bengali *bhadralok*, and other scribal castes with a distinct urban-middle-class orientation. These sections traditionally dominated the bureaucracy and white-collar professions, and their entry into business was essentially a post-Independence development.
- The third pathway he identifies as 'from field to factory', covering those communities classified as belonging to the other backward castes (OBCs), like the Kammas, Reddys, Gounders, Jats, Patidars, Marathas, Nadars, Ramgarhias and others who traditionally worked in agriculture and can be classified as 'rural middle class', and whose political, social and economic empowerment was one of the

epochal features of the last century. Their journey into corporate boardrooms, howsoever uneven across regions, paralleled a similar transition achieved by the urban scribal castes.

Both these urban- and rural-middle-class-led trajectories have undermined the time-honoured association of business communities with an exclusively Vaishya (Bania) order.[4]

Dalit Entrepreneurship

Another recent phenomenon is that the Dalits—which indicates several scheduled-caste communities—are increasingly getting into businesses and entrepreneurship. The Dalit Indian Chamber of Commerce and Industry (DICCI) is playing an important role in this development. Its members are frequently part of pre-Budget consultations. It marks the emergence of a nascent trend in India, of enterprising Dalits choosing to create independent businesses instead of depending on quotas in government jobs to get ahead.

Some Dalit entrepreneurs have built impressive empires, like Kalpana Saroj, who heads Kamani Tubes, with an estimated turnover of Rs 500 crore; and Ratibhai Makwana, whose Rs 300-crore Gujarat Pickers is one of the country's largest polymer distributors. Other Dalit entrepreneurs include Bhagwan Gawai, of the Dubai-based Saurabh Energy DMCC, which supplies petroleum products and petrochemicals, and provides consultancy and support services in the aviation sector; Raja Nayak, who runs enterprises across diverse sectors, including international shipping and logistics, corrugated packaging, packaged drinking water, wellness and chia rice products; and Ashok Khade, managing director of DAS Offshore, an engineering company that builds and refurbishes offshore rigs and platforms.[5]

But DICCI's effectiveness has been challenged, and there is also a debate on whether the business opportunities emerging from globalization have benefitted Dalits more than reservations. Some academics argue that reservations have benefitted Dalits far more than globalization and its business opportunities. But we feel that the process of Vaishyavization of Dalits is far more critical in changing the situation of Dalits than just reservation. It is not either/or as far as reservations and entrepreneurship are concerned, but perhaps both.

Many recent studies have brought out the issue of caste facilitating the emergence of newer businesses in different locations across the country. The role of extended family and caste has been recognized in the upward mobility of middle castes in commerce and business. Hence, the jati or community or caste plays a major role in entrepreneurship and also facilitates the upward mobility of the whole caste rather than individuals. Caste mobility provides newer paradigms for caste members rather than limited reservation in government jobs. Also, entrepreneurship is nurtured and growth is facilitated through caste relationships. Given this reality, this social capital needs to be recognized and celebrated. In a sense, the Vaishyavization process of all the castes will churn society and caste equations will also undergo changes. It will also have implications for politics, which we will explore in Chapter 10.

9

Caste and the Service Sector

In India, the non-corporate sector dominates service activities, which, in turn, constitutes nearly two-thirds of our economy. These are also the fastest-growing activities. So justifiably, it is the non-corporate sector that should be termed 'the engine of our economic growth', and the Indian economy could perhaps be justifiably termed the 'partnership and proprietorship economy', since these kinds of enterprises dominate the service industry.

Further, the growth of the economy from the 1990s onwards should actually be attributed to the partnership and proprietorship (P&P) firms in service activities and not to the reforms carried out by the government or the minuscule contribution of the corporate sector. But, ironically, this remarkable contribution of the P&P sector has not been adequately documented and appreciated.

Whenever the term 'service sector' is mentioned, the immediate recall is the IT sector and companies like Infosys and Wipro. Factually, all software-related activities come under business services, which itself makes up for nearly 5 per cent of our national income.[1] The service sector covers a much larger canvas and is the fastest-growing sector in our economy, generating scope for large-scale employment. The activities which constitute the service sector are mentioned in Table 9.1. It is clear that this sector encompasses diverse activities carried out by large multinationals as well as by small-time entrepreneurs.

Table 9.1
Activities Constituting the Services Sector

(1)	Construction
(2)	Trade
(3)	Hotels and restaurants
(4)	Transport, including tourist assistance activities as well as activities of travel agencies and tour operators
(5)	Storage and communication
(6)	Banking and insurance
(7)	Real estate and ownership of dwellings
(8)	Business services including accounting, software development, data processing services, business and management consultancy, architectural, engineering and other technical consultancy, advertisement and other business services

(9)	Public administration and defense
(10)	Other services including education, medical and health, religious and other community services, legal services, recreation and entertainment services
(11)	Personal services and activities of extra-territorial organizations and bodies

Note: *We have considered 'construction' as part of the service sector in our discussion, even though sometimes it is considered part of the 'secondary sector'. See* Report of the National Statistical Commission, *(NSC) p. 186, Vol. II, August 2001, Ministry of Statistics and Programme Implementation, New Delhi.*

Also, nearly two-thirds of our GDP comes from service sector activities (see Table 9.2A and B). Between 2004–05 and 2011–12, the service sector grew by 17 per cent (at current prices) and 9.8 per cent (at constant 2004–05 prices), and this is much higher than other sectors as can be inferred from Table 9.2A and B.

Table 9.2A
GDP Shares of Different Sectors, 2004–05 to 2015–16
(Current Prices)

Sector	Sector Share 2004–05	Sector Share 2011–12	Sector Share 2015–16[*]
Agriculture and allied activities	19.0	17.5	17.5
Industry	20.2	18.5	21.6
Services	60.8	64.0	61.0
Total	100	100	100

Note: Constructed from National Accounts Statistics, Central Statistics Office (NAS-CSO) data

[*]For 2015–16 it is gross value added, net of taxes and subsidies to GDP

Source: At current prices NAS 2013/2017, CSO, New Delhi

Table 9.2B
GDP Shares of Different Sectors, 2004–05 to 2015–16 (Constant Prices)

Sector	Sector Share in Rs Crores 2004-05	Sector Share in Rs Crores 2011-12	Sector Share in Rs Crores 2015-16*
Agriculture and allied activities	5,65,426 (19 per cent)	7,39,495 (14.1 per cent)	16,17,208 (15.4 per cent)
Industry	6,00,928 (20.2 per cent)	10,30,086 (19.6 per cent)	24,21,302 (23.2 per cent)
Services	18,05,110 (60.8 per cent)	34,74,001 (66.3 per cent)	64,52,004 (61.4 per cent)
Total	2,971,464 (100)	52,43,582 (100)	104,90,514 (100)

Note: *Figures in brackets are percentages to column total*

For 2015–16 it is gross value added, which means net of taxes and subsidies to GDP

Source: *2004–05 and 2011–12 at constant 2004–05 prices, NAS 2013, and 2015–16 at constant 2011–12 prices, CSO, New Delhi*

Between 1950–51 and 1990–91, the share of the services sector in GDP rose by only 13.07 per cent, which is an increase of about 0.33 percentage points per annum. However, between 1990–91 and 1999–2000, the share increased by 7.29 per cent, which is an increase of 0.81 percentage points per annum.[2] Between 2004–05 and

2011–12 it has grown by 17 per cent per annum, i.e., 2.4 percentage points per annum. Clearly, the growth rate has been very significant in these eight years. Further, it has grown by 6.8 percent in terms of compounded annual growth since 2011–12 at 2011–12 constant prices—even though its share has slightly declined.

It is generally accepted that while economic reforms were indeed initiated in the early 1990s, most of the policy changes brought about pertaining to manufacturing and the financial sector related to government and corporate activities. The regulation and control pertaining to service activities were with the state governments, and there were no major reforms in these segments, as we will see later. Hence, it is difficult to ascribe the growth of the service sector, and that of the entire economy during the last two decades, to the reform measures initiated.

The role of the non-corporate sector in certain service activities, listed in Table 9.1, is very significant, spanning construction, trade, hotels and restaurants, non-railway transport, storage, real estate and ownership of dwellings, business services and other services.

Table 9.3

Share of Major Service Sectors in NDP at Current
Prices (Per Cent)

Items	1990–91	2000–01	2004–05	2010–11	2011–12
Construction	6.4	6.6	8.2	8.7	8.6
Trade, hotels and restaurants	14.1	15.6	17.5	18.6	19.5
Transport (non-railways) & storage	4	4.5	5.9	5.5	5.6
Real estate, ownership of dwellings & business services	2.9	6	8.7	10.1	10.6
Other services	6.3	8.7	8.4	8.2	8.2
Total of the above	33.7	41.4	48.7	51.1	52.5

Note: *Computed by the author from NAS data, various issues,
CSO, New Delhi*

Source: *pp. 32–3, NAS 1995, and p. 22, NAS 2005, St. 12 NAS
2013*

These exclude railways, communication, banking,
public administration and defence. The excluded are
predominantly part of the government sector or in the
significantly organized sector (banking, for instance).
Table 9.3 gives the share of these seven major service

sectors in the net domestic product (NDP)[3] for different years. We observe that the share of these seven service sectors in the NDP has consistently gone up, from 34 per cent in 1990–91 to 53 per cent in 2011–12, showing an increase in the role of these activities in the economy during the period, but more particularly in the last two decades.

As pointed out by the National Statistical Commission (NSC), although the service sector plays a pivotal role in our economy, the database of this sector is highly disorganized, since there is no well-organized mechanism for maintaining a regular and proper database. The services sector can be broadly classified into three segments, namely, the public sector, the private corporate sector and the household sector. The first two are considered as organized and the latter consists of unincorporated enterprises, including all kinds of proprietorship and partnership firms run by individuals. The database for the organized sector is mainly made up of published accounts by corporate and government entities.

The NSC also points out that the estimates of gross value added per worker based on the follow-up enterprise surveys of economic census periodically conducted by the Ministry of Statistics and Programme Implementation are often too low. Also, the estimates of the number of workers in different sub-sectors as per these surveys differ widely from those available from other sources like employment and unemployment surveys of the National Sample Survey Office and the decennial population census.

Table 9.4 gives the share of the non-corporate sector in activities like construction, wholesale and retail trade, hotels and restaurants, road transportation and storage, and real estate and business services such as medical services, legal services and so on. We find that the share of the unorganized sector, which is non-corporate in nature, is nearly 75 per cent in trade (wholesale and retail), hotels and restaurants. It is more than 80 per cent in non-railway transport, nearly 65 per cent in construction, more than 50 per cent in storage and more than 60 per cent in real estate and business services.

It is pertinent to point out that the estimates of the non-corporate sector in these activities need substantial improvements. As already noted, the report of the National Statistical Commission (NSC 2001), for instance, points out that the estimates of the non- corporate service sector are based on data that suffer from an inadequacy in terms of sampling frame and sample size.

Table 9.4
Share of Non-corporate Sector in Major Service Activities (NDP at Current Prices per Cent)

Category	1980–81	1990–91	2000–01	2010–11	2011–12
Construction	48	55.5	59.1	62.3	64.6
Trade, hotels and restaurant	89.7	92.2	79.5	77.4	74.2
Transport (other than railways)	65.9	77.7	78.8	80.6	81.4
Storage	67.5	49.4	48.3	48.9	51.6
Real estate, ownership of dwellings & business services	99.5	99.0	77.3	62.2	60.8
Other services	46.2	37.0	29.6	42.6	42.9
Total (share in service activities)	74.4	73.5	65.3	66.5	65.8

Note: Share at current prices

Source: NAS 1997, St 76.1, 2013, Central Statistical Organisation, New Delhi

Unfortunately, for the years after that, the CSO has not provided a break-up between corporate and non-corporate sectors—in terms of organized and unorganized. But we can infer from the non-financial corporation data provided that the proportions have not changed significantly for later years.

Unlike the developed countries, the likes of Walmart, Sears or Marks and Spencer in retail, or Greyhound and Federal Express in transportation, or McDonald's, Burger King and Pizza Hut in restaurants are not as yet the order of the day in India. The size of the non-corporate sector in service activities and the phenomenal growth rates achieved in the last two decades need recognition. As said earlier, the Indian economy can be called the partnership and proprietorship economy or the unincorporated economy. Not only does the non-corporate sector play a major role in service activities, it also has good growth rates.

All along, conventional wisdom has indicated that the accelerated economic growth in the last twenty-five years has been due to the reform measures initiated in the early 1990s by the Narasimha Rao government and continued later by various Central governments. The period after 1992, particularly, is regarded as the 'Reform Era', when Manmohan Singh was finance minister in the Narasimha Rao government. There is also another view held by some economists who claim that the growth rate has actually been increasing right from the 1980s, and, to some extent, the policies of Rajiv Gandhi (post 1984) were instrumental not only in opening up the economy but also in triggering off the growth rate.

Actually, the service sector encompasses a much larger canvas, and it is also the fastest-growing sector in the economy. More importantly, the growth in the economy during the last two decades was due to proprietorship and partnership firms in service activities, like construction, trade (wholesale and retail), hotels and restaurants, non-railway transport, real estate, business and other services.

The real growth rate in the service activities dominated by the non-corporate sector is given in Table 9.5, along with that of agriculture and organized-sector manufacturing. We observe that many of the service activities dominated by the non-corporate sector have grown much faster than agriculture or organized-sector manufacturing. We find that trade has grown by 10 per cent CAGR, real estate, etc., at 10.6 per cent and other services at 8.8 per cent. Actually, the phenomenal growth in construction, trade, hotels and restaurants, non-railway transport and business services are the main reasons for the significant growth of the Indian economy in the twenty-first century.

Table 9.5
NDP/GVA (Gross Value Added) and Growth Rate in different Activities at Constant Prices, 2004–05 to 2017–18 (Per Cent)

Category	Growth rate (NDP) 2004–5 to 2011–12	Growth rate (GVA) 2011–12 to 2017–18
Agriculture and allied activities	3.6	3.1
Manufacturing	8.4	7.2
Of which		
Organized	9.5	-
Unorganized (non-corporate)	6.5	-
Construction	8.4	3.7
Trade hotels and restaurants	9.0	9.7
Of which		
Trade	9.2	10.0
Hotels and restaurants	7.4	6.3
Non-railway transport	7.7	6.6
Banking, insurance and fin. services	15.3	7.2
Real estate, ownership of dwellings and business services	9.0	10.6
Public admin. and defence	8.1	5.6
Other services	6.3	8.8
Total NDP (including other activities)	8.3	6.9

Note: 2004–05 to 2011–12 growth rate is the geometric average growth rate (CAGR) at constant 2004–05 prices of NDP. It is computed from the NAS 2013. The growth rate (CAGR) for 2011–12 to 2017–18 is of GVA at 2011–12 prices.

Source: National Accounts Statistics (NAS) 2013, 2019; Central Statistical Office (CSO), GOI, New Delhi

Table 9.5A provides consolidated data for the pre-COVID period. It shows growth rate from 2011–12 to 2018–19.

It also shows that the CAGR of all service activities that are predominantly non-corporate is higher than that of agriculture and manufacturing sectors. One may note that non-corporate sectors dominated by caste clusters drive our growth.

Table 9.5A
Growth Rates of Gross Value Added at 2011–12 Prices between 2011–12 and 2018–19

Category	Growth Rate (GVA) 2011–12 to 2018–19
Agriculture and allied activities, and mining and quarrying	3.44
Manufacturing/elect/gas and water supply/construction	6.45
Trade hotels and restaurant/transport and communications	8.34
Banking and Insurance and fin. services/real estate and business services	9.29
Community/social/personal services	7.33
Total GVA	6.87

Note: The compounded average growth rate (CAGR) for 2011–12 to 2018–19 is of GVA at 2011–12 prices CSO, GOI, New Delhi, 2018–19 data is a provisional estimate of GVA

Source: Economic Survey 2019–20, Vol. 2, Statistical Appendix, Table 1.3, p. A7, Ministry of Finance, New Delhi, January 2020

It is important to note that the service sector, where non-corporate organizations are dominant, is regulated by rules and regulations of the state governments rather than by those of the Central government. Except for direct and indirect taxes (income tax, GST), all other tax impositions are in the hands of the state governments, and most of the regulations pertaining to the non-corporate sector are under their purview. Some of these regulations are listed in Table 9.6.

Table 9.6
Regulations of Service Activities of the
Non- corporate Sector by State Governments

1. Shops and Establishments Act
2. Food and Adulteration Act
3. Negotiable Instruments Act
4. Road Transport Act
5. Commercial Taxes Act
6. Money Lending Regulations Act
7. Urban Land Usage and Development Act
8. Stamp Duty and Other Registration Charges
9. Acts for the Entertainment Industry
10. Acts Pertaining to Educational /Medical/Religious Institutions, etc.

The instruments to generate taxes from the service activities of the non-corporate sector are also with the state governments. Some of these are included in Table 9.7.

Table 9.7
Instruments of Taxation of the Service Activities by State Governments

Commercial tax (one of the major revenue sources for state governments); now replaced by GST Centre and state
Road tax on passenger as well as commercial vehicles
Tax on IMFL/licence fees on opium cultivation
Tax pertaining to tendu leaf/granite trade
Entertainment tax
Professional taxes
Cess on other activities

After the introduction of the Goods and Services Tax (GST) many taxes listed above have been merged into GST. But still, several others, like liquor tax, petrol, entertainment, land registration, etc., are with state governments. Even though agricultural income tax is under state governments, none of them want to levy it, for political reasons.

None of these acts or regulations have undergone any major reforms or changes in the last twenty years.

More importantly, we observe that caste and community clusters play a major role in the service sectors, particularly in the non-government and non-corporate segments, which can be called unincorporated or partnership and proprietorship activities. These clusters are not like manufacturing clusters, specific to a location, but are spread across regions where the activities take place. We can call them linear clusters. For instance, as previously mentioned, a substantial portion of the retail trade in electrical items in Bengaluru is undertaken by entrepreneurs from the Mewar region of Rajasthan, sometimes called Mewaris. Similarly, in Tamil Nadu, the Nadars and Muslims from Keezha Karai and Koothanallur in coastal Tamil Nadu dominate the retail trade. In restaurants, entrepreneurs from the Mangalore and Udupi regions belonging to the Bunt and Brahmin communities have significant presence in cities like Bengaluru and Mumbai. In the restaurant industry in Tamil Nadu, for instance, the Nadar community has penetrated into different towns. Interestingly, one restaurant chain, called Saravana Bhavan, owned by Nadars, has become a major brand name and has branches in places like Delhi, Malaysia and the USA. The Woodlands chain of hotels, started by a person from the Udupi Brahmin community, is another example.

Malabar Muslims have a large presence in the retail trade in Bengaluru, and in many towns of Kerala and Tamil Nadu. Their presence is both in specific products and in activity lines, like gold, electronic goods stores, as well as in general stores, like supermarkets. The major advantage of these communities is the availability of labour from their villages and market access due to the existing presence of relatives who give them an initial leg-up in the trade.

In construction, we find that the Kammas, Reddys and Kapus from coastal Andhra Pradesh are active, more so in large infrastructural activities. Many construction labourers are from the Chittoor and Khammam areas of Andhra Pradesh, and this gives the entrepreneurs much-needed resources to bid for large-scale projects. There are agents who recruit these labourers and bring them to the project site. The other labour cluster for construction activities is in northern Karnataka.

Education is one area where significant caste clusters have been created in many states. The coastal region in Karnataka has many educational institutions started by the Bunts (Shettys) and Pais, and northern Karnataka has many started by the Lingayats. Actually, it was suggested that the demand for a separate religious tag by a section of the Lingayats was meant to free their educational institutions from the regulations of the government, especially from the Right to Education Act (RTE).[4] This act imposes conditions on enrolling candidates to the extent of 25 per cent, from economic and socially backward sections, at reduced fees, and is not applicable to minority institutions—those which are not Hindu, thereby enabling non-Hindu institutions to charge full fees for those seats. In Maharashtra, many sugar barons belonging to the Maratha community have started educational institutions. In Gujarat, it is Patels and Punjabi Khatris and other Hindu Punjabis. In all these instances, the financing has primarily come from within the community.

In the finance sector, communities from Mangalore in Karnataka have played a major role. All major banks founded in Karnataka, namely Canara Bank, Syndicate Bank, Corporation Bank, Vijaya Bank and Karnataka Bank, were established in or around Mangalore, and developed by communities like the Bunts and Goud Saraswath Brahmins. These were later nationalized in the late '60s. Many of the non-bank institutions in Tamil Nadu, like Sundaram Finance and Shriram Chits, were founded by Brahmins; and others, like the Tamil Nadu Mercantile Bank, by the Nadars; and many by the Chettiars and Gounders.

In the software industry we find substantial numbers of Tamils and Telugus, followed by the Bengalis—a popular joke in Seattle is that Microsoft will even give holidays for Telugu and Tamil festivals. Domestic reservation has also forced some who have been denied opportunities here to migrate.

In the film industry, caste plays a major role— the Kapoor family and their relatives being a good example in Bollywood. In the Tamil and Telugu film industries, often, fan associations are caste-based (based on the actor's caste). The Thevars and Nadars from Tamil Nadu are some of the predominant communities, and they tend to associate with members of their caste working in films, to the extent that there are YouTube videos which give details of the caste of different actors.[5]

In terms of other professions, we find interesting community linkages and migration across countries. In major cities like Bengaluru, Mumbai and Chennai, one finds a substantial number of plumbers from Odisha. It is believed that nearly half the plumbers come from a single district—Kendrapara in Odisha, which houses the State Institute of Plumbing Technology (SIPT), the only institute in the country dedicated to plumbing.[6] Many belong to OBC castes that are closely linked. Similarly, cooks from Odisha—who belong to Brahmin castes—are found in many parts of the country, predominantly in Kolkata.

The beauty parlour and spa industry across the country is dominated by girls from Assam, Manipur, Meghalaya and other north-eastern states, many of whom are STs.[7] In the 1970s, Chinese families began to set up beauty parlours in cities across India, many of them in Kolkata. As the number of these parlours increased, they required more and more beauticians. Women from the North-east, especially from the Khasi tribe of Meghalaya, migrated to Kolkata and eventually moved to other parts of the country.[8]

In all these instances, the prevalent information network among communities helps a lot, and, to some extent, the initial financial advantage is also provided by the caste and community network.

Clearly, the non-corporate sector in the service industry has significant caste clusters across geographical regions. It helps in mobility and information networks, market access, and, most importantly, it helps in risk mitigation.

10

Caste and Politics

Caste organizations were active in politics even in pre-Independence times, particularly in south India. An organization called the South Indian Liberal Federation (the official name of what came to be later known as the Justice Party), primarily composed of the OBCs of the Madras Presidency, was active from 1917. This organization was anti-Brahmin and pro-British in its stance, and even ruled the Madras Presidency for thirteen years between 1920 and 1937. It was opposed to the Indian National Congress and lost to the Congress in the 1937 election.

The Justice Party was formed from this federation in 1944, headed by E.V Ramaswamy Naicker (Periyar), and it observed 15 August 1947 as a mourning day based on its stated stance that after the British left, the country would be ruled by 'northerners' and 'upper castes'.

Post-Independence India adopted universal adult franchise—the system of one person, one vote and first-past-the-post method of winning. In the pre-Independence period, voting was restricted based on income and assets. Interestingly, in India, voting rights to women were given without any debates or opposition. In contrast, in Europe and USA, women secured the right to vote only after protests and agitations.

The introduction of adult franchise gave rise to caste assertions and consolidation based on caste as a common factor. The Socialist Party of the '50s was the first to recognize caste as an important element of Indian society and the need to mobilize the masses based on caste. The communists were more focused on class (economic criteria) as a factor for mobilizing the proletariat.

Ram Manohar Lohia, the then leader of the Socialist Party, recognized caste as a factor for mobilization and focused on the intermediate castes, also known as OBCs. This gave rise to two major developments. One was the integration or homogenization of sub-castes, and the other was the demand for reservation in government services and educational institutions. This communal reservation was already being practised in the southern states where the British had introduced it in the 1930s, based on the 1932 Round Table Conference. This became a clamour all over the country.

First, the government introduced reservation for the constitutionally listed scheduled castes and scheduled tribes, to the extent of 7.5 per cent for STs and 15 per cent for SCs based on their proportion in the population as per the 1931 census. This was done in 1951, after the Constitution came into force through an amendment to Article 15(4).

Consolidation of Castes

As previously stated, the offshoot of adult franchise— one man, one vote—gave rise to the wooing of voters based on caste affinities. Hence, many sub-castes were slowly integrated into a larger caste. Innumerable examples can be given. For instance, in Tamil Nadu, there were three major castes with more than eighty sub-castes. They were known as the Mukkulathors ('Three Kulam' people or three communities). They were the Kallars, Maravars and Agamudayars. Over a period of time, they began to identify themselves as the Thevars. The terms 'Mukkulathor' and 'Thevar' are now used synonymously. According to R. Muthulakshmi of Madurai Kamaraj University, Thevar 'literally means celestial beings or divine-natured people', and Mukkulathor means 'three clans united together'. The three constituent communities of Agamudayar, Kallar and Maravar believe that they share a common origin, based on the myth of the progenitor of their community being the offspring of a relationship between Indra and a celestial woman. Each of the three groups traditionally believes itself to be superior to their fellow Mukkulathors.[1]

While they share a common mythological ancestor, the three communities also claim ancestral differences. The Agamudayar consider themselves to be descendants of the Chera dynasty, while the Kallar claim descent from the Chola dynasty, and the Maravars believe they are related to the Pandya dynasty. In the last forty years or so, the community now known as the Thevars has come to be considered a powerful vote bank in the southern part of Tamil Nadu. The AIADMK Party, led by film actor and politician M.G. Ramachandran (MGR), was supposed to have been fully backed by the Thevars.

There are plenty of similar instances. For example, the Jats, who have more than a hundred sub-castes, are a powerful vote bank in western Uttar Pradesh and have, for long, been supporters of the erstwhile Jat leader and former prime minister Charan Singh and now of his son, Ajit Singh of the Rashtriya Lok Dal. In fact, many political parties in India—particularly the regional parties—are caste-based and family-controlled. One may even term them as unlisted family/caste enterprises. In some states, like Tamil Nadu, every caste has its own party, but all claim that they wish to 'abolish' caste!

Interestingly, a petition was filed in the Supreme Court before the 2009 parliamentary poll to bar regional and caste-based parties from contesting elections to Parliament. The court dismissed the petition at the admission stage itself.[2]

These political parties, numbering around twenty, are mostly caste- or region-based. They are spread from Kashmir to Kanyakumari. Arguably, the largest

party is the Congress, controlled by the Gandhi family.
The others are:

1. National Conference (NC) of Jammu and Kashmir:
    Led by Sheikh Abdullah, Farooq Abdullah and
    Omar Abdullah
2. People's Democratic Party (PDP) of Jammu and
    Kashmir: Mufti Mohammad Sayeed and Mehbooba
    Mufti
3. Shiromani Akali Dal (SAD) of Punjab: Prakash
    Singh Badal and Sukhbir
4. Indian National Lok Dal (INLD) of Haryana:
    Chautala family
5. Jharkhand Mukti Morcha (JMM): Soren family
6. Rashtriya Lok Dal (RLD) of Uttar Pradesh: Charan
    Singh family
7. Samajwadi Party (SP) of Uttar Pradesh: Mulayam
    Singh Yadav family
8. Bahujan Samajwadi Party (BSP) of Uttar Pradesh:
    Mayawati family
9. Trinamool Congress (TMC) of West Bengal:
    Mamata Banerjee family
10. Rashtriya Janata Dal (RJD) of Bihar: Laloo Prasad
    Yadav family
11. Nationalist Congress Party (NCP) of Maharashtra:
    Sharad Pawar family
12. Shiv Sena (SS) of Maharashtra: Thackeray family
13. Telugu Desam Party (TDP) of Andhra Pradesh:
    Chandrababu Naidu family

14. Bharat Rashtra Samithi (BRS, formerly Telangana Rashtra Samithi or TRS) of Telangana: K. Chandrashekar Rao family
15. Janata Dal (Secular) of Karnataka: Deve Gowda family
16. Dravida Munnetra Kazhagam (DMK) of Tamil Nadu: M. Karunanidhi family
17. Pattali Makkal Katchi (PMK) of Tamil Nadu: S. Ramadoss family
18. Marumalarchi Dravida Munnetra Kazhagam (MDMK) of Tamil Nadu: Vaiko and family
19. Desiya Murpokku Dravida Kazhagam (DMDK) of Tamil Nadu: Vijayakanth and family

These twenty families are mostly caste-based and also sometimes promote regional chauvinism. Actually, among the major parties, we can say that the Bharatiya Janata Party (BJP), Communist Party of India, Communist Party of India (Marxist) and Aam Aadmi Party (AAP) are the three which are not controlled by any family and which do represent any single caste. At the state level, the Biju Janata Dal (BJD) of Odisha can also be considered.

The caste-based parties mainly use caste for reservations and also apply pressure for benefits to their caste constituency.

Unincorporated Regional Satraps

The important point to note is not about the national aspirations of these caste-based parties but the functioning of these regional parties and their control. Whether it is the DMK or the Shiv Sena, where the family battles have come into the open; or the Akali Dal, the Janata Dal (Secular), the Pattal Makkal Katchi or the Nationalist Congress Party, where the heir apparent has been anointed; or the Telugu Desam Party, the Rashtriya Janata Dal or the Samajwadi Party, where the entire 'family is tirelessly working'— the issue is the family business called 'caste-based political parties'.

Like in all businesses, we need to delineate the nature of the business model adopted by these family enterprises, aka regional parties. It is important to mention that Tamil Nadu is the pioneer in this aspect, where the interests of the state, party and government are all subsumed for the welfare of a family or caste enterprise. In any business, particularly in corporate organizations and listed businesses, shareholder wealth maximization is the main objective. Since these regional parties are not listed on the stock exchanges, their correct 'market valuation' cannot be estimated.

The total wealth declared by these leaders (including that of their wives) during election time, in the form of affidavits, can be a guide to the net worth of the enterprises. But then, it is usually an undervaluation, since it can only reflect what can be declared and also does not tell the future earning potential of the business. In this, there are multiple stakeholders other than the controlling family that plans, allocates and executes projects where the returns are shared.

Business Units

The family business is conducted through different departments of the government, like education, irrigation, urban development, PWD, power and so on. Some of these business units are low-volume, high-margin centres located in urban development or special economic zones (SEZs), where one project can earn up to a couple of crores. With global companies located in small towns, plenty of new opportunities are created. Other business units, in sectors like elementary education, which is a large-scale transfer industry, are also low-margin but high-volume businesses. Here, every teacher transferred may provide only in thousands of rupees, but the numbers are large. The family also needs to take care of the interests of other families, which are sub-regional or from other caste parties. Hence, allocation of business units plays an important role.

Sometimes, there are differences within the family, like in any other business. The executives (government officials) are transferred according to the requirements of the family. Sometimes, very senior officials become part of the family and integrate well. In this model, note that the business expenses are those of the government, but all the revenues go to the family. It is an interesting win-win model that does not have any comparable international cases. One reason that dynasty politics thrives is the amount of money made in corruption, which is handed over to progeny. Obviously, the ill-gotten wealth cannot be given to 'outsiders' by giving them control of the party.

Competitors

Competition can come from other families, which have their own community of shareholders. There are also dissidents from the current enterprises due to multiple wives or differences among children and so on. The time frame for maximizing the family wealth after one election is specified, which is what differentiates such family enterprises from other regular business models. Due to the short timespan it has, the family can and does become rapacious, and depends on a continuous extraction of higher and higher bribes to meet the greed of the family and friends. The turnover and attrition among supporters is also high, since their aspirations, too, become greater over the course of time. A minister may quit, a leader may defect or create difficulties due to differences. (One can count many examples of this, starting with E.V.K. Sampath, of the DMK in Tamil Nadu, in the '60s, to Narayan Rane from the Shiv Sena in Maharashtra in the '90s, and Siddaramiah from the Janata Dal in the first decade of the 2000s.) Hence the need to create powerful entry barriers as well as exit costs. And the exit cost can sometimes be violent.

In 2018, media reports talked about caste wars in Andhra Pradesh between castes affiliated to different political groupings. Vijayawada was in the grip of a caste war between the Kammas, Kapus and Reddys due to a new political outfit floated by a film actor by the name of Pawan Kalyan, who primarily had the support of the Kapu community.[3]

There are practical difficulties for the national parties to adopt this model, even though post the Indira Gandhi period one observes that the Congress party has been identified with a single family. But India being a vast country, trying to have the national market on a single-family basis is difficult, and we also observe that that the Congress party is shrinking in electoral terms. There is a decline in terms of its seat share in Parliament.

Land as a Scarce Resource

Will the business model of the regional parties based on caste and families ever meet its nemesis? One reason it will flourish for some more years is the increasing importance of land as a factor of production. In the 1960s, capital was scare and land was easily allotted. Now, capital is available even from global sources but land is scarce, and that is the strength of these caste-based outfits. Control of land and allotment of the same is the primary industry. To that extent the family business will flourish, since land is scarce. This has been understood by our regional political parties, and it is a state subject. It is possible that this business model may fail due to sub-regional parties coming up on their own and fragmenting the business. Already, we have a party for the Vanniars and a party for the Nadars in Tamil Nadu, and a party for the Malas in Andhra, the Gowdas in Karnataka and, of course, the Yadavs in UP and Bihar, and one for the Kurmis and Dalits in UP, and for the Jat Sikhs in Punjab, besides others. With further fragmentation of these groupings, many family enterprises will be either on a mergers-and-acquisitions mode or on a small business–smaller reach mode. Such situations can go foul.

Secondly, there is the matter of the greed of some of these families. Due to pressure from multiple controlling interests (say, many wives, many children, extended family and so on), the margins demanded from projects may exceed the cost of running a political party.

Caste as Political Capital

Caste calculations in politics start from the selection of candidates. Most parties rely on choosing a candidate from the 'majority' caste in a constituency (including sub-caste). But then, if every party sponsors a candidate from the majority caste, how do people choose? Most constituencies have 60 per cent voting record out of the total registered voters. So if there are, say, three major contestants, then getting some 25 per cent of the vote may take you to the winning post if the other two opponents split the remaining 35 per cent. Again, to get the votes of the other major castes, one should be perceived as a balanced leader of the major caste but not antagonistic to other castes.

In the 2018 state assembly election in Telangana, it appears that even the Communist Party of India (Marxist) (CPI[M]) relied more on caste factors than class issues, and the central unit of the party was forced to warn the state unit about it.[4]

After the polls, the government formation is also based on caste factors, and both regional and caste factors are balanced in forming governments. All the major castes get representation, and dominant supporting castes get crucial ministries, like finance, home, public works, energy, education, land records, transport and so on. In popular parlance, these are considered 'ATM' departments—'All Time Money'— in terms of corruption, and provide opportunities of bribes being shared among officials and ministers. Family-run caste-based parties try to keep crucial portfolios within the family or the extended family. Not only that, the treasurer of the party is also usually from the family or closely linked to the family.

Interestingly, even major newspapers publish the caste composition of the ministry formed. A report in *The Hindu* about the formation of the Kamal Nath ministry in Madhya Pradesh in December 2018 thought it fit to list the number of ministers belonging to various castes.[5]

Most of the bureaucrats chosen for top positions in various departments are also often chosen on the basis of caste factors, since it is believed that this will facilitate 'smooth functioning' of the processes. Another interesting aspect in many cases is that the caste and the region factors coincide—that is, the major caste is typically concentrated in a couple of districts of a state. This ensures that both caste and regional aspirations within a state are balanced.

A few parties at the regional level, like the Trinamool Congress in West Bengal, are not heavily reliant on caste factors. But they are the exceptions. Most regional parties, like the Janata Dal (Secular) in Karnataka (Vokkaligas), the AIADMK (Thevars), the PMK (Vanniars) and the DMK (OBCs and Muslims) in Tamil Nadu, the TDP (Kammas) in Andhra Pradesh, the Shiv Sena (Marathas) in Maharashtra, the Samajwadi Party (Yadavs and Muslims), the Bahujan Samaj Party (scheduled castes) and the Rashtriya Lok Dal (Jats) in Uttar Pradesh are dependent on caste mobilization for gathering votes.

Caste and Corruption

The previous chief minister of Tamil Nadu, the late J. Jayalalithaa, and her aide, Sasikala Natarajan, were, in the past, convicted by the Supreme Court on bribery charges. Sasikala served a prison term in this regard. Similarly, Lalu Prasad Yadav, the former chief minister of Bihar, is serving a prison term in what is popularly known as the 'fodder scam'. These are illustrations to highlight the prevalence of corruption at the highest level.

The bribe money collected from contractors, truck operators, the land registration process, provision of electricity and water connections, allotment of government land, etc., are used partly for party purposes and partly for enriching families. The need to have reliable ministers from the same caste or extended family is to get a fair share of the illicit money collected. Interestingly, as already indicated, most of these family parties have dynastic succession since the funds would otherwise go into 'external' hands.

Caste networks help in spreading the cheese on a larger slice of bread, so that it benefits more people belonging to one's own caste in terms of appointments, contracts, licences and so on, and this, in turn, would help the party concerned in the next election. Like any other democracy, distributing favours and distributing them along the network is crucial, since these are used as IOUs for the future. The main advantage of caste-based favours distribution is that during elections the IOU can be encashed from the caste leaders.

Demand for Delisting

A unique development witnessed in the state of Tamil Nadu is the Puthiya Tamilagam, a political party representing the Devendra Kula Vellars—who are scheduled castes—wanting to be delisted from the tag.[6] According to reports, Puthiya Tamilagam leader K. Krishnaswamy stated that they did not want to be a part of the list of scheduled-caste communities because they were facing social discrimination.

The community has reportedly stated that reservation breeds stigma, and that they are being looked down upon in society because of their SC status. They also added that over the years, the community has only been treated as a vote bank, and they are now seeking upward social mobility and progress. They do not mind even losing privileges like reservation.

They feel that the removal of the tag will make them more acceptable and give them social status. 'The community doesn't like being called as Pallars or SC or Dalit. This community owned lands and even voted during the British Raj. We should have never been included into the SC category,' said M. Thangaraj, president of Devendra Charitable Trust.[7]

While this is only a small group in India, the nature of the demand is contra-indicative when there is a clamour to be included in the list of weak communities. This is still a nascent movement, but it might have far-reaching implications for caste-based reservations. If it gains momentum, the movement will have significant impact on the polity of our country in the coming years.

The government has recently introduced 10 per cent reservations for the so-called upper castes, based on income criteria. This will breach the 50 per cent ceiling set by the Supreme Court for reservations. The issue is in the Supreme Court, where political parties like the DMK are opposing it, stating that social justice seems to be based only on caste (social and educational backwardness) and not on the economic situation. There is also a clamour to introduce reservation in the private sector to achieve full social justice, and that will have its own cascading effects. We have to wait and see the full ramifications of all these moves with an eye on the 2024 election.

Conclusion

Among the various identities a person carries in India, the caste identity is a strong and powerful one. It has specific 'samskaras' from the time of birth to marriage to death. It facilitates group identity and helps in group activities. It plays an important role in business relationships, more so since our economy is still predominantly a 'relationship-based' economy and not a contract- or rule-based one. It facilitates initial capital formation and credit for doing business and also risk mitigation. Failure is not frowned upon but considered as a process of learning. Caste as social capital plays an important role in the development of economic clusters and acts as an engine of economic growth.

In a way, caste is a unique institution, and in the contemporary situation it is also used for political mobilization. Some argue that there is a need to create a 'casteless' society. Several reformers have attempted it in the last 2000 years. But they have only partially succeeded in reforming the caste system, rather than abolishing it. One criticism of caste is that it is birth-based. But so is religion, except for the fact that you can opt out of it. Even in the case of caste in urban centres, one can opt out or conceal one's caste. But if the layers of identity are lost, then one may be left with only one's legal identity and dealt with only by courts. Interestingly, democracy, through its system of one man, one vote, has strengthened caste identity and has also led to the integration of many sub-castes into a larger caste identity.

At international forums, caste is used as a stick to beat anything connected to Indian religions, customs and culture. In other words, caste is made to be for Indians what the Holocaust is for Germans and Austrians.

Recently, in some US universities like Harvard, caste has been equated to race and discussed under critical race theory, wherein Indian Dalits are equated with Blacks in the USA and Brahmins are considered as Whites. These can have far reaching implications in the political sphere of India, similar to the Aryan invasion theory (now increasingly questioned) of an earlier period.[1]

We have an uncanny ability to be masochistic. But more tragic is our enthusiasm to convert all our strengths into weaknesses, since some White men started to abuse Indians for having the caste system. We fail to recognize that it is a valuable social capital, which provides a cushion for individuals and families in dealing with society at large, and, more particularly, in interactions with the state. The Anglo–Saxon model of atomizing every individual to a single element in a rights-based system and forcing him to have a direct link with the state has produced disastrous effects in the West, where families have been destroyed and communities have been forgotten. Every person stands alone there, in a sense stark naked, with only rights as his imaginary clothes to deal directly with the state. The state also does not have the benefit of concentric circles of cushions to deal with individuals. The state has taken over the role of father and mother as well as spouse, in terms of social security, old-age homes and the rights of children to sue and divorce parents!

Caste has been made a curse by intellectuals on the basis of half-baked knowledge and acceptance of the Eurocentric model of the individual, which is a rights-based rather than a duty-based system. Hence, one way to overcome it is to have reservations, since the Eurocentric model suggests that. If you decide to carry the cross or burden which others impose, then you begin to impose the solution provided by them. In a sense, the debate does not distinguish between caste discrimination and caste as social capital. The cry to abolish caste is to homogenize Indian society, which has been attempted by many reformers, but they have not been successful.

We can surmise that a rigid caste hierarchy was practised after the 1881 census conducted by the

British, which, for the first time, enumerated castes and arranged them in a hierarchy. If caste oppression was really severe in the past, then there should have been many caste wars in the last 2000 years! But history does not provide information about large-scale caste wars.

Swami Vivekananda, in his address at Jaffna in 1897, said, 'The older I grow, the better I seem to think of these [caste and such other] time-honoured institutions of India. There was a time when I used to think that many of them were useless and worthless, but the older I grow, the more I seem to feel a diffidence in cursing any one of them, for each one of them is the embodiment of the experience of centuries.'[2]

Caste has played an important role in the consolidation of business and entrepreneurship in India, particularly in the last seventy years. The economic development that has taken place in India Uninc., in terms of the partnership and proprietorship activities, has been financed by domestic savings, and facilitated by clusters and caste and community networks.

So let us recognize the positive role played by caste as a social capital in the midst of all criticisms of the caste system.

Acknowledgements

A book of this nature owes thanks and acknowledgements to a diverse group of persons who have contributed in no small measure to its fruition.

In 2000, a team of us—Shri S. Gurumurthy, Dr Kanagasabhapathy, C.A. Muralidharan of Coimbatore et al.—undertook a trip to towns like Namakkal, Karur, Tiruppur and a few others to understand the functioning of local credit markets. That was a trigger point for me. Later, some of us visited towns in Karnataka, Gujarat and Punjab. That fieldwork gave an insight into the functioning of economic clusters and the role of caste. For that, my sincere thanks to Shri S. Gurumurthy. The erudite Dr Kanagasabhapathy provided lots of inputs on castes in Tamil Nadu.

I benefitted much from the discussions I had with M.D. Srinivas and J.K. Bajaj of the Centre for Policy studies. Dr Subramanian Swamy and his daughter, Dr Gitanjali Swamy, provided insights about credit markets in various countries. Thanks are due to them.

R. Thiagarajan (founder, Shriram Group) and N. Rangachary (ex-chairman, CBDT and IRDA) are always encouraging and supportive of these initiatives. Mr Murali, of Shriram Properties, is another person who encouraged and provided information.

My previous employer, the Indian Institute of Management Bangalore, provided the right ambience and data sources. My students of several batches, who underwent elective courses on this theme, need special mention for their inputs and probing questions.

SASTRA University, where I am currently a chair professor, provided logistics as well as stimulating discussion opportunities on various issues. Thanks to its former vice-chancellor, R. Sethuraman, and the current vice-chancellor, Dr Vaidhyasubramanian.

Vivekananda International Foundation, Delhi, with which I am associated, deserves special thanks for their support and encouragement.

Thanks are due to my research assistants, Ms Neha and Ms Bhavya, for their help.

Special thanks to Karthik Venkatesh for editing this book and providing important clues about various aspects.

My wife, Usha, should receive special mention here for her patience and support.

Needless to add, the errors and omissions are mine alone.

Notes

Introduction

1. Anuradha, 'Swami Vivekananda on Caste', Hindu Post, 29 May 2017, https://hindupost.in/history/swami-vivekananda-caste/#:~:text=Under%20the%20original%20varna%20system,a%20Vaishya%2C%20or%20a%20Shudra.
2. Aloke Tikku, 'Niti Aayog Panel Has to Deal with 4.6 mn Caste Names in Census', *Hindustan Times*, 19 July 2015, https://www. hindustantimes.com/india/niti-aayog-panel- has-to-deal-with-4-6-mn-caste-names-in-census/story- UL2lEz7tJpn76n1HYgWLxL.htm
3. D.P. Satish, 'Dalits, Muslims Outnumber Lingayats and Vokkaligas in Karnataka? "Caste Census" Stumps Siddaramaiah Govt', News18, 15 March 2018, https://www.news18. com/news/politics/dalits-muslims-outnumber-lingayats- and-vokkaligas-in-karnataka-caste-census-stumps- siddaramaiah-govt-1689531.htm

4. R.B. Bhagat, 'Caste Census', *Economic and Political Weekly*, Vol. 42, Issue No. 21, 26 May 2007, https://www. epw.in/journal/2007/21

5. Kevin Walby and Michael Haan, 'Caste Confusion and Census Enumeration in Colonial India, 1871–1921', *Histoire sociale/Social History*, Vol. XLV, No. 90, November 2012, https://hssh.journals.yorku.ca/index.php/hssh/article/view/40067/36268; and, Asha Krishnakumar, 'Caste and the Census', *Frontline*, Volume 17, Issue 18, 2–15 September 2000, https://frontline.thehindu.com/static/ html/fl1718/17180910. htm

6. M.N. Srinivas, *Some Reflections on the Nature of Caste Hierarchy*, *Collected Essays*, Oxford University Press, 2005, pp. 196–97.

7. Dipankar Gupta, *Interrogating Caste*; Penguin Books, 2000, p. 1.

Chapter 1

1. Sanjeev Nayyar, 'Rethinking Caste: Why We Can't Be So One-Dimensional', Firstpost, 28 January 2013, https://www.firstpost.com/india/rethinking-caste-why-we-cant-be-so-one- dimensional-604681.htm

2. Nanditha Krishna, *'The Equals of Men'*, *Sunday New Indian Express*, 29 May 2006.

Chapter 2

1. Household Assets Holding, Indebtedness, Current Borrowings and Repayments of Social Groups in India (as on 30 June 2002), All-India Debt and Investment Survey, NSS, 59th Round, January–December 2003.

2. National Family Health Survey (NFHS – 2) Key Findings, 1998–99, International Institute for Population Sciences, Bombay, https://www.dhsprogram.com/pubs/pdf/SR81/ SR81.pdf

3. Charu Soni, 'How Reservations Help Disadvantaged-Caste Students Get Higher Education', India Spend, 20 July 2016, http://archive. indiaspend.com/cover-story/how-reservations-help-disadvantaged-caste-students-get-higher- education-88852

4. Shoba Warrier, 'Only 5-10% Benefitted from Reservation', Rediff, 8 October 2015, http://www.rediff.com/news/interview/only-5-10-benefitted-from-reservation/20151008.htm

5. Jayaprakash Narayan, 'A New Edifice for Reservations', *The Hindu*, 2 September 2015, https://www.thehindu.com/opinion/lead/a-new-edifice-for-reservations-scheme/ article7604312.ece

6. Rakesh Basant and Gitanjali Sen, 'Who Participates in Higher Education in India? Rethinking the Role of Affirmative Action', IIMA, November 2009, https://web.iima. ac.in/assets/snippets/workingpaperpdf/2009-11-01Basant.pdf

7. Mihika Basu, 'OBC Candidates Break Quota Barrier: 4,085 in Common Merit List', *Indian Express*, 20 June 2014, https://indianexpress.com/article/india/india-others/obc-candidates-break-quota-barrier-4085-in-common-merit-list/

8. K. Ramachandran, 'Going "Forward" in Medical Admissions?', *The Hindu*, 23 August 2004, https://www.thehindu. com/2004/08/23/stories/2004082308900400.htm

9. Ibid.

10. www.tnhealth.org/index.php

11. https://realitycheck.wordpress.com/2015/06/21/analysis- of-tamilnadu-mbbs-admissions-2015-16/

12. Manasa Rao, 'Should Poor among Forward Castes Get Reservation? Madras HC Judge Rakes up Debate', News Minute, 18 December 2017, https://www.thenewsminute.com/article/should-poor-among-forward-castes-get-reservation-madras-hc-judge-rakes-debate-73356

13. https://twitter.com/YuvarajPollachi/status/1591449140101513216?s=20&t=QxH-VV9t-U7BtzHhfN1UPQ

14. R. Vaidyanathan, 'Reservation in Engineering Jobs', 2 October 2022, https://rvaidya2000.com/2022/10/02/reservation-in-engineering-jobs/

Chapter 3

1. 'India Has a Workforce of 47.41 Crore: Government', *Economic Times*, 16 July 2014, https:// economictimes.indiatimes.com/news/politics-and-nation/india-has-a-workforce-of-47-41-crore-government/articleshow/38486047.cms

2. *The Economic Survey 2021–22*, Chapter 10, p. 372.

3. Principal status (PS) measures the activity in which an individual has spent relatively longer time of a reference year (major time criterion), while subsidiary status (SS) measures the activity status of an individual who has spent majority of days out of workforce but has worked for a short period of time (more than thirty days). Usual status is the activity status of a person during the reference period of 365 days preceding the date of survey.

4. *The Economic Survey 2021–22*, Chapter 10, p. 373.

5. R. Vaidyanathan, *India Uninc.*, Westland, 2014.

Chapter 4

1. Sanskritization denotes the process by which castes or tribes placed low in the caste hierarchy seek upward mobility by emulating the rituals and practices of the upper or dominant castes.

Chapter 5

1. 'What Is Social Capital? OECD Insights: Human Capital', OECD, https://www.oecd.org/insights/37966934.pdf
2. Ibid.
3. Robert D. Putnam, *Making Democracy Work: Civic Traditions in Modern Italy*, Princeton University Press, 1994.
4. Gurcharan Das, *India Unbound: From Independence to the Global Transformation Age*, Penguin Books, 2002, p. 150.
5. Émile Durkheim, *The Division of Labor in Society*, Free Press New York, 1997, p. liv.
6. Francis Fukuyama, *Trust: The Social Virtues and the Creation of Prosperity*, Simon & Schuster, 1996.
7. Swaminathan S. Aiyar, 'Social Capital—An Idea Whose Time Has Come', *Times of India*, 28 May 2000.
8. Robert D. Putnam, *Bowling Alone: America's Declining Social Capital*; 'An Interview with Robert Putnam', *Journal of Democracy*, 6:1, January 1995, pp. 65–78, http://xroads.virginia.edu/~HYPER/DETOC/assoc/bowling.html
9. B. Bolin, E.J. Hackett, S.L. Harlan, A. Kirby, L. Larsen, A. Nelson, T.R. Rex, S. Wolf, 'Bonding and Bridging: Understanding the Relationship between Social Capital and Civic Action', *Journal of Planning Education and Research*, 24, 2004, pp. 64–77.

10. R. Muthulakshmi, *Female Infanticide: Its Causes and Solutions*, Discovery Publishing, 1997, pp. 11–13.
11. Krzysztof Iwanek, 'Counting Castes in India', Diplomat, 5 August 2016, https://thediplomat.com/2016/08/counting-castes- in-india/
12. Aloke Tikku, 'Niti Aayog Panel Has to Deal with 4.6 MN Caste Names in Census', *Hindustan Times*, 19 July 2015, https://www. hindustantimes.com/india/niti-aayog-panel- has-to-deal-with-4-6-mn-caste-names-in-census/story- UL2lEz7tJpn76n1HYgWLxL.htm

Chapter 6

1. *All-India Report of Sixth Economic Census*, http://www.mospi.gov.in/sites/default/files/economic-census/sixth_economic_census/all_india/9_ChapterIV_6ecRep.pdf
2. R. Vaidyanathan, *India Uninc.*, Westland, 2014.
3. Dimitris Georgarakos and Sven Fürth, 'Household Repayment Behavior: The Role of Social Capital, Institutional, Political, and Religious Beliefs', Goethe University, Frankfurt, and CFS Goethe University, Frankfurt, March 2010, https://www.sciencedirect.com/journal/european-journal-of-political-economy/vol/37

Chapter 7

1. P. Kanagasbapathy, *Indian Models of Economy, Business and Management*, third edition, Prentice Hall India Learning Private Limited, 2012.
2. Indian Clusters, Definition of Cluster in the Indian Context, http://laghu-udyog.gov.in/clusters/clus/ovrclus. htm

3. *Report of the Working Group on Clustering and Aggregation for the Twelfth Five-Year Plan,* Department of Industrial Policy and Promotion, Ministry of Commerce and Industry, Government of India, October 2011, http://planningcommission.gov.in/aboutus/ committee/ wrkgrp12/wg_aggregation.pdf

4. *Report of the Working Group on Micro, Small and Medium Enterprises Growth for 12th Five-year Plan (2012-17),* Ministry of Micro, Small and Medium Enterprises, New Delhi, http://www.dcmsme.gov.in/ working_group2012.pdf

5. *SME Clusters in India, Identifying Areas of Intervention for Inclusive Growth,* Institute for Studies in International Development, April 2010, http://planningcommission. nic.in/reports/sereport/ser/ser_sme1910.pdf

6. *Manual on Energy Conservation Measures in Ice Making Cluster Bhimavaram,* Bureau of Energy Efficiency, https://beeindia.gov.in/sites/default/files/Bhimavaram_ Ice Making_APITCO.pdf

7. Peter Knorringa and Khalid Nadvi Khalid, 'Rising Power Clusters and the Challenges of Local and Global Standards', *Journal Of Business Ethics,* January 2016 https://link.springer.com/article/10.1007/s10551-014-2374-6

8. P. Kanagasabhapathi and M.N. Arunkumar, 'A Study of Sankagiri Transport and Thiruchengodu Rig Industry', April 2005.

9. Ibid.

10. B. Balasubramanian, R. Srinivasan and S. Vaidhyasubramaniam, 'Social Capital and Consumption Smoothing: Narrative Study on 'Moi Virundhu' (Community Feast for Fund) a Unique Community Practice in Rural Thanjavur District, Tamil Nadu, India', *European Journal of Social Sciences,* Vol. 30, Issue 3, May

2012, http://www.europeanjournalofsocialsciences. com/issues/ EJSS_30_3.htm

Chapter 8

1. *World Development Report 2002: Building Institutions for Markets*, World Bank, 2002, p. 175.
2. Abdul Hafiz Lakhani, 'Gujarat - Hub of Kite Industries, Muslims Are in Front Business', 9 October 2014, http://www.maeeshat.in/2014/10/gujarat-hub-of-kite-industries- muslims-are-in-front-business
3. Sumangala Damodaran and Pallavi Mansingh, 'Leather Industry in India', CEC working paper, Centre for Education and Communication, New Delhi, 2008, http://www. cec-india.org/libpdf/1437550410LeatherIndustryinIndia. pdf
4. Harish Damodaran, *India's New Capitalists*, Orient Blackswan, New Delhi, 2009.
5. 'Breaking Caste Barriers: Stories of 5 Dalit Entrepreneurs Who Reached the Top', Your Story, 25 January 2018, https://yourstory.com/2018/01/dalit-entrepreneurs/

Chapter 9

1. C.P. Chandrashekar, 'How Significant Is IT in India?', *The Hindu*, 31 May 2010, https://www.thehindu.com/opinion/columns/Chandrasekhar/How-significant-is-IT- in-India/article16304607.ece
2. Rangarajan report, National Statistical Commission, 2001, p. 186.
3. The net domestic product (NDP) equals the gross domestic product (GDP) minus depreciation on a country's capital goods.

4. 'Educational Institutions Run by Lingayats to Benefit', *The Hindu*, 19 March 2018, https://www.thehindu. com/news/national/karnataka/educational-institutions-run-by- lingayats-to-benefit/article23296164.ece
5. This is just an illustrative example. There are a number of other such videos: https://www.youtube.com/ watch?v=wnKcSIshBfA
6. Namrata Sahoo, 'Flush with Cash: Inside the Unofficial Plumbing Capital of India', *Caravan*, March 2016, https://caravanmagazine.in/lede/flush-with-cash-unofficial- plumbing-capital-india
7. Divya Sreedharan, 'The Business of Looking Good', *The Hindu*, 11 May 2013, https://www.thehindu. com/features/magazine/the-business-of-looking-good/ article4698602.ece
8. Sanjukta Sharma, Mayank Austen Soofi and Pavitra Jayaraman, 'The North-East Complex', *Mint*, 25 August, 2012, https://www.livemint.com/Leisure/ foRapqgPiyjHmti5VfNKzM/The-NorthEast-complex. Html

Chapter 10

1. R. Muthulakshmi, *Female Infanticide: Its Causes and Solutions*.
2. 'Keep LS Out of Bounds to Regional Parties: PIL', *The Hindu*, 18 April 18 2008, updated 9 October 2016, https:// www.thehindu.com/todays-paper/tp-national/Keep-LS-out-of-bounds-to-regional-parties-PIL/article15205977.ece
3. 'Vijayawada in Grip of Caste-War between Kammas, Kapus and Reddys', *Deccan Chronicle*, 22 April 2018, https://www.deccanchronicle.com/nation/politics/220418/

vijayawada-in-grip-of-caste-war-between-kammas-kapus-and-reddys.html

4. Sobhana K. Nair, 'CPI(M) Reprimands Telangana Unit for Projecting Candidates on Caste Lines', *The Hindu*, 23 December 2018, https://www.thehindu.com/ news/ national/telangana/cpim-reprimands-telangana-unit/ article25813875.ece

5. Anup Dutta, 'Madhya Pradesh CM Kamal Nath Expands Cabinet, Inducts 28 Ministers', *The Hindu*, 25 December 2018, https://www.thehindu.com/news/ national/madhya-pradesh-cm-kamal-nath-expands-cabinet-inducts-28-ministers/article25826859.ece

6. Pon Vasanth B.A., 'Take Us Out of SC List or Face Unprecedented Protests', *The Hindu*, 6 May 2018, https:// www.thehindu.com/news/national/tamil-nadu/take- us-out-of-sc-list-or-face-unprecedented-protests-puthiya-tamilagam-virudhunagar/article23795791.ece

7. Udhav Naig, 'Amit Shah to Back Devendrakula Vellalars as One Community', *The Hindu*, 21 July 2015, https://www.thehindu.com/news/national/tamil-nadu/ amit-shah-to-back-devendrakula-vellalars-as-one-community/article7445470.ece 69

Conclusion

1. Rajiv Malhotra and Vijaya Viswanathan, *Snakes in the Ganga: Breaking India 2.0*, BluOne Ink, 2022.

2. Swami Vivekananda, *Lectures from Colombo to Almora*, http://www.ramakrishnavivekananda.info/ vivekananda/ volume_3/lectures_from_colombo_to_ almora/vedantism.htm